ARTHUR'S BRITAIN

The Land and the Legend

Text by
DEREK BREWER

Photographs by
ERNEST FRANKL

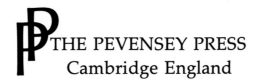

THE PEVENSEY PRESS
Cambridge England

Published by The Pevensey Press
6 De Freville Avenue, Cambridge CB4 1HR, UK

Photographs: Ernest Frankl, except those in the Introduction: reproduced by kind permission of the Curators of the Bodleian Library, Oxford

Maps: Carmen Frankl

Edited by Ruth Smith

Designed by Kate Hughes-Stanton
Design and production in association with Book Production Consultants, Cambridge

© Ernest Frankl and The Pevensey Press, 1985

ISBN 0 907115 26 8

Typesetting by Cambridge Photosetting Services
Printed and bound in Italy by New Inter Litho, Milan

Frontispiece: The entrance to Portchester Castle (see p. 83)

A name in CAPITAL LETTERS indicates that there is a separate description elsewhere in the book, to be found by reference to the list of contents.

Contents

Introduction

'Arthur lives!' makes a good motto to start with, for he lives in our minds and hearts, and by the imprint of his legends far and wide on the British landscape. We see the landscape differently when we see it in the light of legend; the legends take on new life when seen as expressions of the landscape. *How* Arthur lives, and where, and if he was ever actually a real man in the flesh, are further questions which have provided interest and entertainment for over a thousand years.

Arthur lives in many stories and episodes told not only of him; he is a magnet to stories and to other heroes with their own stories. These tales are lodged in many corners of Britain –and indeed in Europe, which is beyond our scope here. There is no doubt that Arthur is British in origin, though British in a sense rather different from the current one. The land of Britain holds a series of peoples, sometime enemies to each other, but all eventually intermingling as successive waves of immigrants have covered the land, working and loving it, enriching it with their blood and bones, and summing up their feelings for it in many stories.

It seems natural to ask first, was there really an 'historical' Arthur? But that represents a modern materialist approach: of course there was – or were – such a man or men (and we shall come back to the 'historical' Arthur), but it is more useful to ask first what the stories about Arthur are, and to explore their richness before looking for the few grains of verifiable historical 'truth'. Whether the stories claim to be histories or folktales does not much matter. They are all creative, mixtures of ancient memories and new inventions, of old and new desires and necessities.

One thing is certain: the earliest stories about Arthur are Celtic, and Arthurian legends are thickest where, of the many layers and mixtures of the British people, the Celtic layer is nearest the surface – on the fringes of the English heartland, from the Edinburgh region across to Strathclyde, in Wales, and in the south and south-west, from Winchester to Devon and Cornwall. Arthur is a dominant figure to whom all sorts of adventures happen, but the earliest references that survive are

Merlin, from a manuscript (Bodleian MS Douce 178, fo. 189v) written in the fourteenth century in Northern Italy but in French, in double columns, with many miniatures and illuminated capital initials, which contains the story of the Holy Grail and then the history of Merlin. These are prose versions of an original verse composition attributed to Robert de Boron, who lived around 1200. Robert invented much of the Grail story in connection with Joseph of Arimathea (see GLASTONBURY). He also invented much about Merlin, telling how he was born of a virgin and a succubus and knew all past and future events. As a magician Merlin advised King Utherpen- dragon, and fostered the king's son, Arthur. Another writer tells that he disappeared after Arthur's death. Here he is seen riding on one of his innumerable journeys.

in Welsh poetry, and the most notable, in the Black Book of Carmarthen (a manuscript of about 1200), refers to his death: 'An eternal wonder is the grave of Arthur.' This enigmatic phrase implies both his greatness and some mystery about his death. Another poem, in the Red Book of Hergest (a manuscript of about 1400, containing earlier material), celebrates a battle and refers to the death of his brave men. Other poems in the same and other early manuscripts refer equally briefly to his sons. In the Black Book there is a poem which contains a dialogue between Arthur and his gatekeeper, mentioning names which become familiar in later stories (for instance Kay and Bedivere), and there are hints of battles and references to Edinburgh and ARTHUR'S SEAT there. Arthur's band is a collection of heroes with fantastic qualities which enable them to slay all kinds of monsters. These stories and references are in manuscripts of the thirteenth and fourteenth centuries, but the stories themselves are centuries older, going back possibly to the fifth or sixth century.

In the Book of Taliesin, a manuscript of about 1275 – Taliesin supposedly being a Welsh poet of the same date as Arthur (that is, living in the sixth century) – a poem called 'The Spoils of Annwfn' seems to describe a dangerous voyage by Arthur and his men in his ship Prydwenn, to a city which represents Annwfn, the Celtic Otherworld, to carry off the magic cauldron of the Otherworld. This voyage appears again, this time successfully accomplished, in the Welsh poem 'Culhwch and Olwen' (in *The Mabinogion*), where Arthur obtains his named sword. Here the Otherworld becomes Ireland.

'Culhwch and Olwen' is a fascinating mish-mash of a poem, deriving from many sources. The hero Culhwch has to win the beautiful Olwen, daughter of a giant, and visits Arthur's court to seek help. This court is a strange miscellany: Arthur himself is the sovereign prince of Britain and the ruler of far-flung lands; his country is Wales, but his court, where he goes to bathe and rest, is at Kelliwic in Cornwall. Saints of Ireland beg for his protection. He has a named ship, mantle, sword, shield and dagger, and a grotesque collection of companions, but no Round Table. He accomplishes bold deeds, the great episode being his pursuit of the wild boar, Twrch Trwyth. This is geographically explicit: the boar runs from Ireland to Porth Cleis near St David's, through South Wales, across the Bristol Channel into Cornwall, and then back into the sea, where he escapes.

The way stories get settings, and settings inspire stories, is shown in another Welsh poem, 'Rhonabwy's Dream', which was probably composed in the thirteenth century but which uses ancient folktale elements. Here Arthur fights the battle of Badon, helped by Kay and by Cador earl of Cornwall. The fantastic events have a solid geographical setting in Powys, which comprises most of central Wales, but Arthur's home is in Cornwall. Some of this material comes from the pseudo-historian Geoffrey of Monmouth, but much is traditional.

Other stories occur in the Welsh poems called Triads (compositions based on three names, with epithets or brief

logrer anla graunt bretaing

te g les fortirer de chrestien

et ad chasteim schastel a serie

danrellehers · er ater le

9

comments) preserved in manuscripts of the thirteenth century or later but much older in origin. Arthur is mentioned frequently. He is the great defender of the country, the hero of strange quests. Also mentioned are Medrawt's (Mordred's) raid on Arthur's court at Kelliwic and his violent treatment of Gwenhwyfar (Guinevere, Arthur's wife), which lead to the battle of Camlann. Another Triad mentions the 'Three Mighty Swineherds', of whom one is Drystan (Tristan), who guards the swine of March (the King Mark of later story); this tradition probably originated in South Wales. Also mentioned in a Triad is the hero Gwalchmei (Gawain), who is known from other texts, often as the son of Arthur's sister. (To be sister's son is a special relationship in archaic societies.)

There are further Arthurian allusions in other poems. *The Gododdin* is a Welsh poem of great antiquity which survives in only one (thirteenth-century) manuscript. It derives from the time in the sixth century when the people we call the Welsh were a tribe established around what is now Edinburgh, and describes a raid against the encroaching English and a battle at Catterick in Northumberland, where the Welsh heroes, though defeated, fight bravely; of one Gwarddur it is said: 'he glutted [?] black ravens on the rampart of the stronghold, though he was not Arthur'. There is no further mention of Arthur, but the poet evidently assumes that he is well known as a great hero.

Another Welsh poem mentions a dialogue between Arthur and his wife Gwenhwyfar (Guinevere), while Merlin is referred to in still others, whose stories may be ancient, though the manuscripts date from as late as the thirteenth or even the fifteenth century. In them Merlin (or, in the Welsh form, Myrddin) is claimed to have lived, like Arthur, in the sixth century. At first he was an independent figure, a mad, wild prophet living in the Caledonian Forest, suffering loss of his lord and his friends in some great battle. But from the twelfth century onwards stories about Merlin were drawn by the magnetic power of the figure of Arthur, so that he became the mysterious wizard who caused Arthur to be fostered in secrecy, and ultimately a prophet whose prophecies were doomed to be disregarded.

If Arthur had not existed he would have had to have been invented. He, or perhaps several great men like him, probably lived in the late fifth and early sixth centuries, when the Celts in Britain, having driven their own Celtic predecessors over to the west, or enslaved them, were themselves subject to the same invading process by the Saxons, that is, the English. So layer after layer of peoples and stories became imposed upon the landscape, each generating legends of struggle, triumph and disaster, with the land as it were reflecting or recalling for later inhabitants all these human excitements and tribulations. With regard to one invasion, which became part of the Arthurian legend, a fourteenth-century poet wrote of the 'founder' of Britain, Felix Brutus (the 'fortunate Brutus'), after whom Britain was thought to be named:

On many a hillside full broad he settled
    with joy,
Where war and wrack and wonder
At times have dwelt therein,
And oft both bliss and blunder
Full swift have shifted since.
                    (*Sir Gawain and the Green Knight*, 14–19)

Chroniclers and other historical writers, who hardly recognised the difference between folktale and history (which is indeed difficult to do), recorded a famous 'British' (i.e. Welsh) commander who resisted the English for some time with success. The first witness is Gildas: writing in about 545 a Latin diatribe *De Excidio Britanniae* ('Of the Destruction of Britain') against the degeneration of the British, then as always a favourite topic, he tells how a successful Briton temporarily stayed the English tide at the battle of 'Mons Badonicus' (about 500) – and the whereabouts of 'Mount Badon' has ever since been a favourite subject for debate. Gildas gives no name to the victor, but perhaps it was a Romanised Briton called Aurelius Ambrosius, whom he elsewhere mentions favourably.

Arthur is first named as a great leader, not a king but a general (*dux bellorum*), in a *Historia Britonum* written in Latin in the ninth or tenth century. The work has been attributed to one Nennius, about whom little more is known than his name.

In Nennius, as befits an historian, the land and the legend come more closely together. Twelve battles are attributed by him to Arthur, and their places named; the twelfth is the battle of Mount Badon (see p. 86 below). In some manuscripts of Nennius' work certain marvels concerning Arthur are placed in South Wales. In Buelt, we are told, is a pile of stones, and on the top a single stone with the footprint of a dog on it, made by Arthur's dog Cabal in the hunt after the wild boar, Twrch Trywth. Sometimes men carry the stone away, but it is always found back in its place next morning. Another marvel is a burial-place beside a well at Ercing (Herefordshire). This is the tomb of Arthur's son Anir. Arthur himself killed and buried Anir there. However often you measure the burial mound it is always of a different size. (Unfortunately neither of these places can now be identified.)

The chronicle called *Annales Cambriae* ('Annals of Wales'), which dates from the tenth century, mentions the battle of Badon and gives it the date of 518; it also records the later battle of Camlann, in 539, when Arthur and Medraut were killed. How they died, and what their relationship was, are not told. The death of the great leader, a mysterious connection with Medraut, and some particular place, are the seeds of the later stories, perhaps derived from the fine blossoms of earlier legends now forever lost.

Arthur as king flowers in the twelfth century, when, in about 1125, the great historian William of Malmesbury refers to the absurdity of the Welsh legends about him but thinks him nevertheless a mighty king who defended his people and won the battle of Mount Badon. William also refers to the tomb of Walwen (Gawain), nephew of Arthur, which was found upon the seashore in the time of William the Conqueror. The place is now known as Walwyn's Castle, near Milford Haven in Pembrokeshire. The tomb of Arthur is not to be found, says William, and hence old songs say he will come again.

Belief in the return of Arthur was passionately held in Cornwall, as we learn from a narrative written in about 1146 by a Frenchman, Hermann de Tournai, concerning a visit to Devonshire by some canons of Laon in 1113. They were told that they were in Arthur's land, and were shown Arthur's Oven and Arthur's Chair – natural features of the landscape. The canons were carrying a shrine of Our Lady of Laon and were on a fund-raising trip, offering miracles of healing by the shrine. At Bodmin a cripple with a withered arm came to be healed and maintained that Arthur still lived. When one of the party from Laon took leave to doubt this an ugly quarrel broke out. The church filled with armed men, and it was only with difficulty that the leader of the canons prevented bloodshed and extricated them. Our Lady of Laon was displeased and the cripple was not healed, though he had presumably had the satisfaction of being supported by his friends in his beliefs. Arthur here, as so often, is firmly if mysteriously located in Cornwall.

Records begin to multiply in the twelfth century, and either because ancient stories are now being noted for the first time, or because new stories are invented, or both, there is from now on an increase in the references to and stories about Arthur.

There are some Latin saints' lives written late in the eleventh or early in the twelfth century which give a rather less glamorous view of Arthur, but which develop the connection of the land with the legend. The Life of St Cadoc tells how Cadoc's father, fleeing from a king in Brecknock with whose wife Gwladys he has run off, comes to three mighty heroes gambling on a hill –none other than Arthur with Kei (Kay) and Bedwyr (Bedivere). Arthur immediately falls in love with Gwladys, but Kei and Bedwyr remind him that he should help the weak and distressed, so nothing comes of it. The Life of St Padarn tells how a *tirannus* ('chieftain') called Arthur comes in his wanderings to the saint's cell, sees and desires his tunic and, being refused, tries to steal it. He is seen by a disciple, who tells St Padarn, who in turn asks that the earth should swallow Arthur – which it does, up to the chin, so that he has to ask pardon. The Life of St Gildas, late in the twelfth century, tells the story of how Melvas, king of 'a warm region' (which seems to indicate Somerset), carries off Guennuvar (Guinevere) and keeps her at Glastonbury for a year. Arthur gathers armies, but St Gildas makes peace and Guennuvar is returned.

So the stories grew, sometimes because a place-name was interpreted as referring to an Arthurian story, or because a striking natural feature attracted the fabulating imagination, or because a particular place wished to associate itself with Arthur. The outstanding example of this last is GLASTONBURY.

Camelot. There was once a Flemish manuscript of the late fifteenth century written in French in double columns telling the story of an Arthurian hero, Guiron le Courtois. It was so beautifully illuminated that someone cut out the illustrations, which are all that survive, now bound up in this manuscript (Bodleian MS Douce 383, fo. 12v) with other material. The original manuscript probably belonged to a Count of Nassau. The story of Guiron consists of a series of fights, ambushes and abductions. Guiron and his lady are cast into prison, where she dies giving birth to his child. Eventually Lancelot, greatest of Arthur's knights, rescues Guiron and the child. In this picture we are shown Arthur with his knights at Camelot, which is depicted as a fine tall fortified city in late-fifteenth-century style, entered by a great gate, and surrounded by meadows.

Comment le roy artus mist leditx
le seneschal a raison, Et des cho
ses quil lui dist .

A ceste partie

Pꝛ dit li contes que lendemain de penthe couste sift li roys artus uenir deuant lub tous ceus qui auoient este compignon de la queste: et quant il furent assis li uns deles les autres les autres il apela les rois ꝛ les

To understand Glastonbury's prominence we have first to note the great boost given to Arthurian legend, and its location, by Geoffrey of Monmouth, who seems to have been of Breton blood and to have lived in Oxford. A great deal has been written about him and his work, the *Historia Regum Britanniae* ('History of the Kings of Britain'), and though its importance is more literary than our concerns here, we should look at what he had to say.

Geoffrey finished his book in about 1135, and it was a tremendous success throughout Europe. He gathered up legends, used extant historical writing and invented a great deal. Like all storytellers he wanted to make his story convincing to his audience, and he reflected the ethos of the dominant Anglo-Norman feudal aristocracy. He traces the line of the kings of Britain from Felix Brutus (mentioned p. 10 above), whom he describes as the grandson of that Aeneas who had escaped from Troy and founded Rome. Brutus came to the island of Albion,

14

killed the giants who occupied it, and made it his kingdom; it was renamed 'Britain' after him. Arthur is one of the latest of a long line of kings, and Geoffrey fits him into a sequence provided by earlier historians concerning the advent of the Saxons, or English. After Vortigern, who fought against the Saxons Hengist and Horsa, came Aurelius, who, advised by Merlin and with his help, amongst other good deeds set up Stonehenge. Aurelius was poisoned by a Saxon, and his brother, Utherpendragon, succeeded to the throne, continuing the fight against the Saxons.

Geoffrey now really takes off. He tells the story of how Uther falls in love with Ygerna, the wife of Gorlois earl of Cornwall. Gorlois angrily leaves the court and retreats to the castle of Tintagel in Cornwall, followed by Uther with an army. Uther, by Merlin's magic, assumes the appearance of Gorlois and so is able to make his way to Ygerna's bed and beget Arthur; Gorlois is killed and Uther marries Ygerna. Thus Arthur has a hero's strange conception and ambivalent status; but where did Geoffrey get his story? In essence it is traditional – many a hero, even Jesus, has a strange conception. Geoffrey's source, if he had one, is unknown, and perhaps his greatness was his capacity to invent traditional, even mythic, events. Yet one can also say that Arthur's known greatness, combined with his mysterious death, required that he should be supernaturally conceived. This is more than history: ordinary life has love, adultery, bastards, death and tragedy in plenty, but a story gives them a pattern, makes sense of them. The story of Arthur gathers together many such elements, sets them in known places, gives them meaning.

Uther and Ygerna also have a daughter, called Anna by Geoffrey. After Uther's death Arthur is crowned, at the age of fifteen. In Geoffrey's account there is no secret upbringing by Merlin, no magic sword in the stone. Later the magnetic power of the story attracts these motifs from earlier legends or from the imaginations of storytellers working traditional themes.

Geoffrey knew the Western Marches, as well as the southwest of England. The ruins at Caerleon-upon-Usk prompted him to place Arthur's court there; he also knew Winchester, Salisbury (near Stonehenge), and something of Cornwall. He was able to pick and choose among the stories available or to invent, like others before and after, and could work out where various events were said to have, or should have, taken place.

Arthur wins great battles and marries the beautiful Guinevere, who is descended from a noble Roman family. Mordred, in Geoffrey's work, is Arthur's nephew, not the illegitimate product of an incestuous union with his sister, as in a later development of the story (or later re-creation of a more ancient tale): the conception of a villain, like that of a hero, requires at least a touch of strangeness. Geoffrey tells how Mordred captures Guinevere when Arthur is in Gaul on his way to attack Rome. As soon as Arthur hears of Mordred's treachery he returns with his army, fights and defeats Mordred at Richborough and again at Winchester, then pursues him into

Cornwall and finally kills him at the River Camblan. But Arthur himself is mortally wounded and carried to the Isle of Avalon, so that his wounds may be cared for. According to Geoffrey this happens in 542. Constantine, son of Cador duke of Cornwall, succeeds to the throne, and soon the history of the Britons blends into that of the Saxons.

Geoffrey had a passion for placing events and a talent for picking up, or inventing, significant episodes. In his *History* Arthur's death is told in a line or two (and Avalon barely mentioned), so he expanded this part of the story in a later work, his *Life of Merlin*. There he gives the poet Taliesin a speech describing how, after the battle of Camlann (Camblan), he and his comrades took Arthur in a ship to Avalon (the Isle of Apples), where the beautiful lady Morgen received them with honour. She put the king on a golden bed in her room and said she would cure him of his wounds if he stayed with her.

The king's greatness is certain, as is his passing; his death is not so sure. Is his passing the same as his death? Many later (or earlier) storytellers thought not. The theme of the ambiguities of death is a rich one for men's minds to play over. Hence the importance of 'Avalon'. Where and what is Avalon?

Welsh sources know only that Arthur's grave is unknown. But Avalon may have been suggested by the Welsh word *afellenau* ('apple trees') and associated with the classical island of the Hesperides, of golden apples, all mingling to create a Celtic Otherworld from which Arthur might return. There is a description of such a place in Geoffrey's *Life of Merlin*; and some people called Glastonbury Avalon in the twelfth century.

In the twelfth century the idea of Arthur attracted loyalties from Celt, Saxon and Norman. All could identify with him to some extent, as with the land which he and they inhabited. His greatness and his mysterious death make up the very image of human life as each of us feels it in ourselves.

Several other motives of very different kinds worked towards a less mysterious passing of Arthur. The more closely we identify with our heroes, the more we want to know about them and where they went:

> And did those feet in ancient times
> Walk upon England's mountains green?

We like to see their footprints upon our own earth; could we but see them themselves! Yet even to see their burial-places asserts that they have been here. Tombs are shrines, and may have the gift of life-giving miracles. Our literally down-to-earth selves make pilgrimages to the resting-places of the great departed dead, who are both here and not here, and may even thus help us. What fascination burial-places have for us: Westminster Abbey draws some of its numinous power not only from the graves of the known and great, but also from the tomb of the Unknown Soldier. Who would not wonder where Arthur's grave might be – wonder and search?

Another motive for seeking Arthur's grave was more particular. Not everyone wanted Arthur back. Plantagenet

Tristan, *a picture (fo. 3) in the late-fifteenth-century Flemish manuscript which tells the story of Guiron le Courtois (see illustration on p. 13). Tristan appears because some French writers fitted the story of Guiron in between the story of Tristan and that of the Grail. Many knights were attracted to Arthur's court by his prowess, fame and goodness. Of these knights one of the very greatest was Tristan, whose story is told below (p. 26). The illustration shows the arrival of Tristan at court, where he is received by Queen Guinevere and her ladies.*

Or6 dist lhistour
que quant trist
tan se fut party
de la damoiselle
si comme ie vo9
ay compte il cheuaulcha tant quil
vint au chastel dessus la mer ou

la royne dillande demouroit et
vseut et brangian Et il y vint de
nuit tout a escient Car il ne vou
loit pas que lon le congneust si
descendy deuant vng prapel Et
osta ses armes et les mist delez
vne fontaine et atacha son cheal

kings, fearing a Welsh rebellion, had no enthusiasm for a possible rival called Arthur, which was one reason why King John had the little Prince Arthur (significantly so named) put to death in 1203. The 'Breton hope', as it was called, of Arthur's return was strong in the twelfth century; Plantagenet kings had good reason to keep Arthur quiet in his grave.

This is where Glastonbury comes in. Henry II, going on the advice of an old British bard, suggested to the monks of Glastonbury that perhaps Arthur's grave was there. Glastonbury Abbey was certainly a very ancient holy place. Moreover, it was going through a period of financial hardship. A sacred shrine to which pilgrims resort is a lucrative possession for any monastery; and even a place of tourist interest is highly desirable. Arthur, if not exactly a saint yet (he became one in some Breton churches in later centuries), had almost divine status.

Although Henry's suggestion was not acted upon immediately, it began to be thought that Arthur had been a patron and benefactor of the abbey. Giraldus Cambrensis, in *De Principis Instructione* ('Of the Education of a Prince'), records that Arthur's grave was discovered in Glastonbury Abbey in 1190 or 1191. It lay deep in the ground, with the great bones of a man, the bones of two wives, a lock of a woman's golden hair and an identifying inscription. Giraldus sees Glastonbury as Avalon, for Glastonbury had once been an island in a lake.

But Arthur could not die, tomb or no tomb, and he became ever more certainly a hero of the whole people. Even in 1191, the very time of the discovery of the grave, King Richard I the Lionhearted presented Arthur's sword, then called Caliburnus, to King Tancred of Sicily. The tomb was opened again by Edward I in 1278, and the bones removed as relics. Eventually the tomb was placed before the high altar, where it was seen between about 1534 and 1539 by Leland, the antiquary, with an epitaph in Latin concluding with the phrase *rex quondam rexque futurus* ('the once and future king').

To this story must also be added that of the Glastonbury Thorn, brought there by Joseph of Arimathea after he had received the blood of the dying Jesus in a chalice and taken down his body from the Cross. The Holy Grail in some accounts was this same chalice. Glastonbury became a place to visit, and a great new church was built.

After Geoffrey of Monmouth the stories of Arthur, and of heroes associated with Arthur, rapidly developed throughout Europe. But that is matter rather of literary history than of the land and the legends, which live at a different level of our minds. Those few heroes who survive in company with Arthur seem mostly to have their roots in Celtic folklore. Lancelot, for example, who has no Celtic root and who was mainly invented by the great French narrative poet Chrétien de Troyes at about the same time as Arthur's grave was being discovered, never became such a figure in the popular imagination as were, at least for a time, the ancient Celtic heroes Cei (Kay), Bedwyr (Bedivere) and Gawain.

Much of the fascinating history of the story of Arthur is henceforth concerned with literary rewritings. Geoffrey of Monmouth had lifted the figure of Arthur from the realm of folklore and the mainly oral poetry of a defeated race and placed it in the world of literacy, education, courtly literature, political history. This literary tradition is not our primary concern here; yet there was a constant interaction between folktale and written literature and history, for the attitudes of mind involved were not always very different. Chrétien de Troyes derived some inspiration, no doubt, from Geoffrey of Monmouth, but very much more from Breton storytellers, as well as from classical Latin literature and other sources. Other poets and prose-writers followed Geoffrey and Chrétien right through the Middle Ages, remodelling and inventing. It was a French poet, Wace, translating and adapting Geoffrey in octosyllabic verse in the late twelfth century, who first mentioned the Round Table, either inventing it or picking up some folkloric reference. The Round Table soon became a metaphor for Arthur's company of knights, but the idea filtered back into folklore so that natural features, or, for example, the Roman amphitheatre at CAERLEON, were thought to be the Round Table. The idea also moved into courtly circles, along with tournaments and jousting for ladies' favours, with the result that some lord, or king, actually had a Round Table made. It now hangs like a vast dartboard in WINCHESTER GREAT HALL.

The writings and interactions came to a climax in the superb work of Sir Thomas Malory, whose *Le Morte Darthur*, finished in 1469–70 and published by Caxton in 1485, is a kind of summary of all the Arthurian tales he could associate with the birth, life, acts and dolorous death and departing of Arthur. Malory's work was popular in the sixteenth and early seventeenth centuries and began to be revived in the nineteenth century when, with Tennyson's help, it gave a new impetus to Arthurian legend.

Malory was a great writer. In summarising Arthurian stories he seized and emphasised their ancient intrinsic essence, mingling romance and pseudo-history. Within the tradition he invented a good deal, like all traditional writers, but he did so in such a way as both to develop and to respect the stories. Though he was a writer, he had something of the folk imagination, and, like Geoffrey, he had a passion for the naming of places and the exact localisation of events. Thus he, and he alone of the Arthurian chroniclers, names the castle of WANDLEBURY near Cambridge. When he settles his hero Lancelot at a castle called Joyous Gard, he tells us that some men say it was ALNWICK and some BAMBURGH (two castles quite near each other in Northumberland). For Malory the story of Arthur is very much the story of England, of England's glory and tragedy, set on England's earth.

We ourselves must take a larger view and see Arthurian story as part of the story of Britain, with its Celtic roots. It would be possible to take a wider view still, but that would mean travelling with the story to Brittany, France, Germany, Italy – further afield than the boundaries of this exploration.

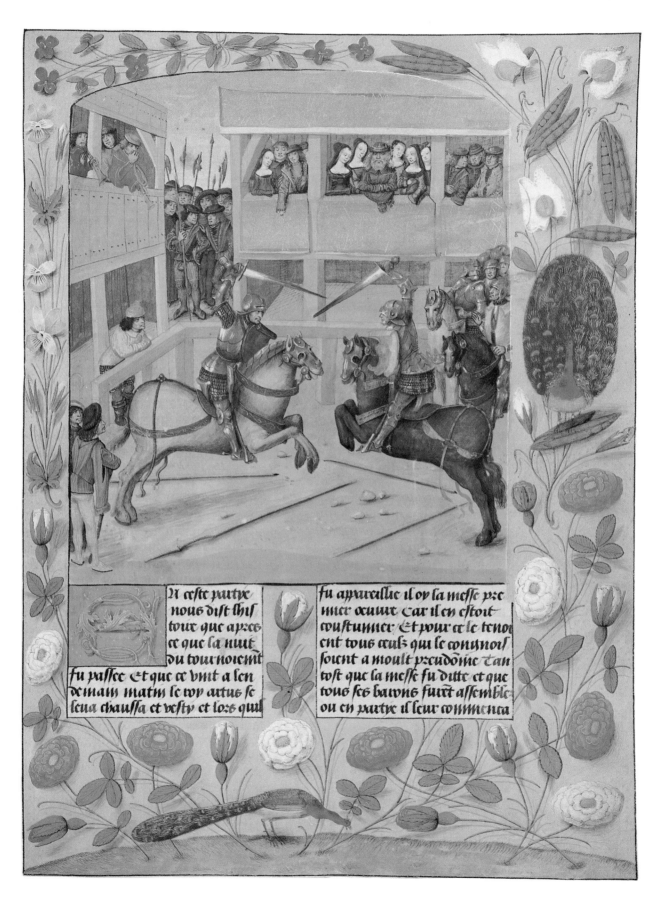

A ceste partye
nous dist lhis
toire que apres
ce que la nuit
du tournoient
fu passee et que ce vint a len
demain matin le roy artus se
leua chauffa et vesty et lors quil

fu appareillie il oy la messe pre
mier œuure car il en estoit
coustummier et pour ce le teno
ent tous ceuls qui le conoissoi
soient a moult preudome tan
tost que la messe fu dicte et que
tous ses barons furent assemble
ou en partie il leur commenca

While the basis of the stories is in Celtic history and folklore, the stories themselves often have a universal appeal, and they moved back across the country from west to east, especially as the English began to identify themselves with the chivalric Arthur, and as Arthur became a national hero to all those who lived on the island. The spreading process culminated in the nineteenth century. There, on a literary level, Tennyson was bold enough in his *Idylls of the King* to parallel Arthur in some respects with Albert the Prince Consort himself.

The collection of localised Arthurian legend by antiquaries had begun in the sixteenth century with Henry VIII's antiquary Leland and the Elizabethan antiquary Camden, who both identify CADBURY CASTLE in Somerset with Camelot. Again this process culminated in the late-nineteenth-century interest in folklore, when most of the current local legends were first collected or created. (Scholars of that time shared much of the credulity, generosity and inventiveness of folk imagination.) At Cadbury several local legends were collected in the 1890s, and a visiting party of antiquaries was asked by an old local man if they had come to take Arthur away from his place under the hill.

Traditional stories grow, change, sometimes decay. The story of Arthur is still being assiduously re-told in the late twentieth century, often on the basis of a much fuller historical knowledge of what life was like in Britain in the fifth and sixth centuries, though seen through disillusioned or cynical late-twentieth-century eyes. The Welsh hero–god, with some grotesque characteristics, became the defender of his people; he modulated into the medieval and Victorian chivalric ideal, variously expressed; in most modern fiction Arthur is portrayed as a barbarian warrior.

Not everyone has taken a favourable view of Arthur. The earliest Welsh stories give him that curious knock-about quality which often belongs to primitive heroes and demi-gods, together with powers far beyond those of ordinary men and a liberal allowance of violence and immorality which also transcends normal human limitations. On the other hand, in the saints' lives the secular hero is often put down with equal violence and a touch of comedy by those Welsh saints who are the ecclesiastical counterparts of secular heroes and just as legendary. The less respectful portrayal of the folkloric Arthur is matched at a literary level in some of the medieval French romances (for example, *Perlesvaus*), which show Arthur in a poor light, failing in the duties of strong leadership.

For political reasons English kings in the thirteenth and fourteenth centuries not only modelled their jousts and entertainments on Arthurian romance, but also made Geoffrey's *History* the basis of a serious claim to overlordship of Scotland. The Scottish in consequence began to take a poor view of Arthur. From the chronicler John Fordun in 1385 to the historian Hector Boece in 1527, they blackened Arthur's character: he was regarded as illegitimate, and Mordred, son of King Loth and of Arthur's legitimate sister Anna, was seen as the rightful king. Scottish poets followed suit. It may be for this reason that

A Joust. The late-fifteenth-century Flemish manuscript from which the illustrations on pp. 13 and 17 are also taken shows (on fo. 16) a splendid tournament at Arthur's court, with two knights jousting against each other, watched by ladies and to the accompaniment of music. The knights wear plate armour of the fifteenth century. They had first run against each other with great spears couched under the right arm and laid transversely across the horse's neck. Here we see that the spears have broken, and now the knights slash at each other with swords, the horses themselves joining in the fight.

Scottish folklore occasionally shows Arthur in a less than complimentary light, though that may also be because it derives from the rough-and-tumble levels of the folk imagination, and from reminiscences of the earliest Welsh stories. the English, however, remained faithful in their allegiance to their former opponent and future king; and in the fifteenth century the University of Cambridge – since Oxford University claimed to have been founded by King Alfred – asserted that its own founder was the even more ancient and glorious Arthur.

Here we are in the charming realm of fantasy, but we may return to the possibility, even the likelihood, of a seed of historical truth – to the possible existence of a real heroic man, a leader of his people. When the English began the raids which developed into an invading immigration, mainly from the south and east, there was certainly resistance from the tribes of Romano-British Celts who then occupied the land, having previously driven out their predecessors and submitted to Roman rule. There is no doubt that there was a temporarily successful Romano-British commander called Ambrosius Aurelianus. There is some likelihood that there was a battle of more than purely local significance at the beginning of the sixth century which gave the English a substantial set-back – the battle of Mount Badon. Where Mount Badon may be is not quite anybody's guess. There are several places in south-west England in which the place-name element *Bad-* appears, as for example in Badbury Rings. Mount Badon seems not totally fabulous.

On the other hand, there were British (i.e. Celtic) kingdoms all around – from the Gododdin, centred on what is now Edinburgh, across Scotland, down England, in what is now Wales, and down into Devon and Cornwall. They fought against each other, as well as against English and Picts. The very earliest traditions of Arthur seem to come from the north (some of them perhaps deriving from Ireland, the ultimate place of origin of the Scottish Celts). According to Adomnán's Life of St Columba, the Irish missionary to Scotland, there was a ruler of Dalriada (the present Argyll and Kintyre) who had a son called Artuir who was slain in battle, and he may have been the, or a, northern Arthur, for the name 'Arthur' in its various forms is rare before the twelfth century.

Another interesting association with the north is found in the *Annales Cambriae* ('Annals of Wales'), which is the first work to record Arthur's death at the battle of Camlann. Among other places suggested as being the site of Camlann is BIRDOSWALD on Hadrian's Wall in Northumberland, for this was known in Welsh as 'Camglann'; but of course the same name is often given to several different places.

We can move away from the north to alternative evidence. A very early Welsh genealogy referring to the rulers of Dyfed, or Pembrokeshire, names an Arthur who would have lived at the right time, around 500. It may be that the English at this period had come to a pause in their expansion, meeting the rougher

Arthur Returns. *The same late-fourteenth-century North Italian manuscript that is illustrated on p. 9 contains (fo. 309) another decorated capital initial letter, whose smallness rather limits the size of the ship in which Arthur is shown returning to England. Medieval artists, like modern ones, were not interested in the ordinary realism of correct proportions. The artist concentrates on Arthur, and shows him crowned and solemnly determined, the waves and the ship being only notionally sketched. Arthur is returning from his conquests in Europe to fight what will be his final battle, against Mordred's treachery at home.*

mer el retoz de la pe
tamgne

urindrent en la bloie
gne. 7 fi tost com il fi
ue en leur cheuax fir

Welsh terrain, and perhaps discouraged by losing a battle against the Britons commanded by a doughty leader. This might be the battle of Mount Badon, somewhere near Wales, after which the English made no further moves westwards for a while. Then the English later came under pressure from more English coming in from their European homeland. This pressure may have caused them to renew their attacks some decades after the battle of Mount Badon; they may have forced their way down into Cornwall, where they eventually defeated the ageing Celtic leader. The wealth of legend about Arthur, especially about his death, in south and south-west England may reflect this, though a similar set of circumstances could have obtained much further north.

The uncertainty of the evidence (of which only a sketch has been given here) need not disconcert us. We all know of real instances of heroic leaders, of national or local success and disaster. There were surely plenty of striking men and events in the sixth century which found no fame at all. But one man, one set of events, somehow caught the imagination of peoples, and in him are combined the greatness, the glories and the tragedy of many other real men, 'our fathers that begot us'.

The stories of Arthur continue, and we continue to cherish them. Not all our legends are ancient, even when they embody motifs of ageless antiquity. The creativity of legend will not die, provided we do not smother all Britain, including our own imaginations and the vivifying sense of the past, under asphalt and brick and plastic. Let the land of Britain live, and Arthur will live too.

South-West Britain

The very earliest localisations of still-recognisable Arthurian places in the south-west are recorded by the canons from Laon already mentioned (*Introduction*, p. 12). They saw Arthur's Oven and Chair between Exeter and Bodmin, but there is no surviving Arthurian legend attached to what maps still name King's Oven (near Merripit, high on Dartmoor). Moving into Cornwall we come particularly to legends of Arthur's death, and it may well be imagined how, as the English pressed down into Cornwall, ancient memories of desperate battles and lost causes, of treachery and tragedy, lingered long, centring on the final battle of 'Camlann', often identified now with SLAUGHTER BRIDGE.

The story of the death, or at least the passing, of Arthur, could not but require some identification of the place where the magic symbol of his power, the sword Excalibur (or Caliburn), strangely received, was mysteriously received back into the waters of death and life. LOOE POOL and DOZMARY POOL are both fitting locations.

Contemplation of the passing of Arthur also requires some consideration of his deeds and origin. Stories of his exploits, of a fairly primitive kind, abound in the lives of Celtic saints who made their way to Somerset, Devon and Cornwall from Wales. These stories are perhaps from the deepest level of Arthurian folklore, and some are grotesque, even a little comic – certainly not solemn.

The variety, drama and beauty of the warm valleys, the high bleak moors, and the dramatic rocky coasts, make these parts extraordinarily attractive and suggestive. They have long been inhabited, as the ancient tombs, and the ruins of monasteries and castles, still show. Many wild adventures have taken place, many incursions and invasions have been suffered or repelled; many saints, themselves as tough as pirates, have toiled to make men better, or have mortified their own flesh for the spiritual betterment of mankind.

The rough bold cliffs of TINTAGEL, confronting the mysterious sea, are the perfect setting for the conception of Arthur the hero–king. Here in Cornwall the Celtic magic is strong at the meeting of land and sea. Further still to the west, over the horizon, lies Ireland, land of violent Celtic passion and romance, while south and west lies that other 'little Britain', Brittany, also the home of ancient romance. The meeting of land and sea at the rocky coast echoes the meeting of this world with the Otherworld, felt so strongly by the Celtic races.

The feeling for Arthur's own presence here, on the high moors near Bodmin, or down in the valleys by the fatal River 'Camlann', reminds us of the grim and constant reality of conquest and tragedy. The story of Arthur is also a story of struggle for the possession of the land by warring races, who have left their blood upon the earth and amongst the peoples.

Earthy passions also surface here. King Utherpendragon's infatuation with Ygerna, wife of Gorlois earl of Cornwall, begins the story of Arthur, their son, as it ends, with sexual deceit. Yet the magic of Merlin allows Uther to impersonate Gorlois, so that Ygerna's faithfulness to her husband is not questioned. In Malory's fifteenth-century version Gorlois is killed before Uther meets Ygerna, so that she is innocent even of unintentional adultery. In this respect the sequence of story-tellers has developed the ancient story. Malory turns the warrior–hero into the chivalric king, with an unblemished mother. But Malory see Mordred as Arthur's illegitimate son, whom Arthur begets on Morgause, his half-sister, before he marries Guinevere. Arthur does not know that Morgause is his half-sister, yet Mordred is thus the product not only of an illicit union but of incest. This throws a darker shadow on the tale of Mordred's treachery to Arthur and his abduction of Guinevere. Mordred is the later name for the Welsh Medrawt, who, according to legend, was Arthur's enemy in the last battle fought in the south-west. It is as if Arthur had to return to the land of his birth to find his death.

Cornwall is also associated with Tristan and Iseult, whose love and death is one of the great medieval stories, frequently told in modern times and the subject of Wagner's famous opera *Tristan und Isolde*.

Tristan comes as a stranger to the court of King Mark of Cornwall, which is regarded as a kingdom contemporary with Arthur's. Tristan's accomplishments win him favour at court and it is revealed that he is Mark's nephew. He kills the champion Morholt from Ireland who has come to demand a tribute of Cornish youths. Later Mark sends Tristan to win him a bride in Ireland, and after many adventures he finds Iseult. When he is escorting her back to Cornwall they both accidentally drink a love-potion meant for the king and Iseult on their wedding-night. The love-potion binds them indissolubly together in love, and in their passion all other obligations are forgotten or disregarded. On her arrival in Cornwall Iseult is married to Mark, and in order to conceal her loss of virginity, she persuades her maid Brangain to take her place secretly in the royal bed. She then plans to murder Brangain to make sure the secret is kept; but she repents. The lovers meet when they can, and the king becomes suspicious. On several occasions he nearly discovers them but is tricked. At last the lovers run away to the forest, where for a while they live an idyllic life. Mark

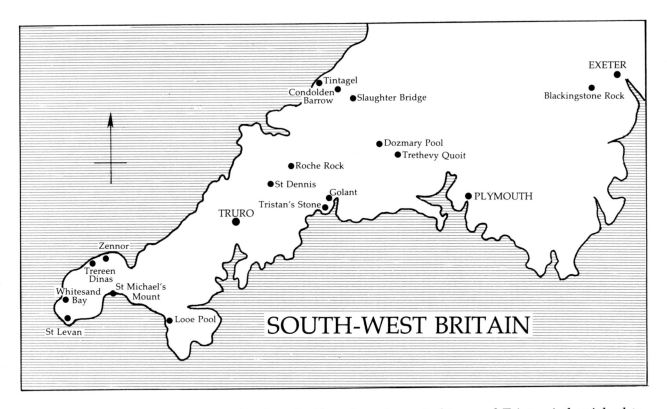

SOUTH-WEST BRITAIN

forgives Iseult, who returns to him, and Tristan is banished to Brittany, where he is persuaded to marry another Iseult, called Iseult of the White Hands. But the marriage is not consummated. After many other adventures Tristan is dangerously wounded and sends for his true beloved, Iseult of Ireland, to come and heal him. It is arranged that if she comes the ship will carry white sails, if not, they will be black. She does come, but Tristan's wife is jealous, and tells him on his sick-bed that the sails are black. He dies, and when Iseult of Ireland finds him dead she herself dies.

The setting of the story is divided between Cornwall, Ireland and Brittany, and there are only a few traces of it in Britain (see ST SAMPSON'S CHURCH, TRISTAN'S STONE, ROCHE ROCK, ST MICHAEL'S MOUNT). It is a story of obsessive love, and of the conflict between passion and society; love and death are closely associated. Sometimes Mark's kingdom is identified as the land called Lyonnesse, which was thought to extend beyond Cornwall, and is now sunk beneath the sea. The story of Tristan is ultimately Celtic, but folktales of other traditions are woven into it. On a rough day on the Cornish coast it is not hard to imagine the pining lovers and the dangers they endured.

These romantic landscapes find worthy counterparts in the Arthurian stories they bear witness to.

Tintagel

The promontory at Tintagel is at the heart of Arthurian legend. The narrow, broken connection of the wild headland with the everyday mainland, the cliffs jutting out into the wide sea, with Ireland over the horizon, are images of the human imagination itself confronting the unknown with speculation, expectation and fear.

On this remote Cornish headland was placed the strange story of the begetting of Arthur (see below). The earliest Welsh stories associate Arthur mainly with Cornwall, whose rocky coast seems to mark the margins of existence: birth and death, the passages of mystery, fear and promise. Tristan too, the Cornish knight, was eventually connected with Tintagel by legend (see pp. 26–7 above).

To visit it today, once the cluster of vulgar modernity in the village has been left behind, is to experience primitive feelings aroused by striking natural scenery and the sense of men living in times long past. Local legend connects this spot with the payment of human tribute in ancient times. Whether or not with historical justification, the legend expresses the coastal feeling of threat from beyond the sea, of danger and cost and of the need of the young to voyage forth. Here may be some source or echo of the story of how Tristan slew the Irish champion Morholt, who came every seven years to demand a tribute of boys and girls from the Cornish king.

The earliest historical evidence is provided by the ruins, dating perhaps from the fifth or sixth century, of what may well have been a Celtic monastery. Celtic Christianity had a taste for desolate sites beside the sea. This settlement, to judge from the remains of pottery, which would have been used to carry wine and oil imported from the Mediterranean, was of some wealth and status. It may have been a stronghold, not a monastery – or perhaps it was both.

Some early Welsh writers locate Arthur's court at 'Kelliwic' in Cornwall, sometimes identified with Castle Killibury (near Wadebridge), an Iron Age camp. A Frenchman, Hermann of Laon, reports that nine canons of his city were told Arthurian tales in Cornwall in 1113. It was more than a foreigner's life was worth in Cornwall in the twelfth century to deny that Arthur would come again. The land was alive with the legend. Hence perhaps Geoffrey of Monmouth's placing of Arthur's birth in Tintagel in his *History of the Kings of Britain*, completed about 1136. The actual castle, part of whose ruins can still be seen (to the right in the picture opposite), began to be built about 1140 by Reginald earl of Cornwall, who was related to Geoffrey's patron, Robert earl of Gloucester.

The place-name Tintagel contains the Cornish word *din* ('fort') in its first syllable; the origin of the rest of the name is not known. Geoffrey's reference seems to be the earliest record, but he did not invent the name, so there may well have been a fortress here for many years, certainly well before Reginald's new castle. The name could derive from the possibly monastic foundation of the fifth century.

Ancient heroes are wonderfully conceived. The story of Arthur's conception, as first told by Geoffrey, is undoubtedly a doctored version of folktale, and introduces Merlin the magician. Geoffrey relates how King Utherpendragon, while entertaining Gorlois duke of Cornwall, fell madly in love with Gorlois' wife, Ygerna, the most beautiful woman in Britain. In anger Gorlois withdrew to Cornwall and the king followed with a huge army, ravaging the country. Gorlois placed his wife in the safest of his castles, Tintagel, while he occupied a fortified camp, 'Dimilioc' (sometimes identified with Tregeare Rounds, an Iron Age fortification some five miles south-west of Tintagel). While Utherpendragon's army besieged Dimilioc, Merlin, to allay the king's suffering, changed his appearance by drugs so that he

exactly resembled Gorlois. Thus he entered Tintagel, deceived Ygerna and begot Arthur. Meanwhile Gorlois himself was killed in battle, so Utherpendragon was able to marry Ygerna. Arthur was not technically the fruit of adultery, since the innocent Ygerna, although she did not know it, was already a widow when he was conceived. Malory opens *Le Morte Darthur* with this story, vividly adapted from an intermediary French source, *Le Suite du Merlin*. Tintagel does not appear again in Arthur's own story. When Arthur was born Merlin fostered him.

Later versions of the story in French, and as told by Malory, make Tintagel the principal castle of King Mark, who holds his court there, and it consequently figures frequently in Malory's story of the lovers Sir Tristram and La Beale Isoud, the nephew and the wife of Mark. But Tintagel eventually fades out of the story as Malory tells it, and Tristram and Isoud finally flee together to Lancelot's castle, Joyous Gard. Other legends placed the tomb of Tristram, and sometimes that of Isoud, in Tintagel. An imaginary tour of Arthurian sites, written between 1350 and 1368 by the Italian Fazio degli Uberti, refers to 'Tristano's' tomb in Tintagel, from which ivy had grown.

Modern fancy has given Arthurian names to rocks on the headland –Arthur's Chair, for example; and in the chasm between the headland and mainland (now traversed by the causeway road) a gigantic footprint of Arthur used to be pointed out. Such are the normal activities of the romantic popular imagination which we all share. Naming of this sort is similar to, if usually less poetic than, ancient legends about places. It humanises the landscape and makes it significant; it need only be judged according to its success.

Under the headland is a great cave which forms a natural tunnel from one side to the other, and which the tide fills. This is called Merlin's Cave and is sometimes associated with the birth of Arthur, who, in Tennyson's account, came magically to Merlin from the sea. This account makes use of another ancient motif where heroes, such as the first Beowulf in the poem of that name, come mysteriously from afar. Cave and sea are picturesque and moving images of birth.

SX 049891   OS 200
5 miles NW of Camelford, on the cliffs behind the village of Tintagel

Condolden, or Cadon, Barrow

Long barrows, when placed, like Condolden Barrow (near Camelford in Cornwall) or Belas Knap (in the Cotswolds), on the top of a great hill, commemorate with numinous simplicity the mighty dead. Once they were the scenes of a whole tribe's mourning, and of the ritual sacrifice of men, women and children to accompany the great chieftain, along with his treasures, in his solemn passage to another world. Ghosts (barrow-wights, as Tolkien calls them) or ambiguously dangerous shape-shifters, such as the Knight of the 'Green Chapel' (itself a long barrow) in the English Arthurian poem *Sir Gawain and the Green Knight,* are often associated with barrows. These usually contain stone burial-chambers, which are sometimes all that remain, as at TRETHEVY QUOIT.

Barrows naturally attract the sense of awe created by the presence of death, the sense of mystery created by the passage of many centuries – they far antedate Arthurian story. But grave-monuments need a name, and Condolden or Cadon Barrow has by local tradition been adopted as the grave of Cador duke of Cornwall.

Cador appears as one of Arthur's heroes in the twelfth-century Welsh poem 'The Dream of Rhonabwy' (as does Drystan, i.e. Tristan), but that may be due to Geoffrey of Monmouth (see below). In an eleventh-century Life of St Carannog, Arthur stays with a chieftain called Cato, who may be Cador; and St Carannog is the patron saint of St Crantock's in Cornwall (see DUNSTER CASTLE). Geoffrey of Monmouth probably picked up something from the tales which lie behind such narratives and invented and rationalised the figure of Cador as one of Arthur's principal supporters. He seems not to be of as ancient origin as Gawain, Kay or Bedivere, and he did not capture the imagination of the later romancers as did Lancelot.

In Geoffrey's *History of the Kings of Britain* Cador fights successfully against the Saxons for Arthur, serves as Arthur's swordbearer, is once called King of Cornwall, and, most importantly, has brought up Guinevere, the descendant of a noble Roman family, in his household. She is the most beautiful woman in Britain, and Geoffrey mentions, quite casually, that Arthur marries her. (The Cador Limenich who dies at the battle of Camblan seems to be a different Cador.) The Constantine to whom Arthur passes the crown (according to Geoffrey, in the year 542) is the son of Cador duke of Cornwall. Cador himself fades from the stories, but this noble barrow high above the sea between Camelford and Tintagel, so near to so many Arthurian places, may well be named the grave of Arthur's sturdy faithful supporter.

SX 091872   OS 200
3½ miles N of Camelford, reached by an unclassified road turning N off the B3263

Slaughter Bridge

Slaughter Bridge crosses the River Camel just north of Camelford in Cornwall. 'Camel' is an old Celtic name for a stream, combining a Cornish word for 'crooked' and a Welsh word for 'stream'. The name is first found in the *Annales Cambriae*, historical Latin records about the Welsh, put together in the tenth century but perhaps using material from the ninth. The *Annales* date 'the Battle of Camlann, in which Arthur and Medraut [= Mordred] fell' in 537. Geoffrey of Monmouth places the battle on the 'River Camblan in Cornwall', and since at least the sixteenth century local tradition has placed Arthur's final battle in the water-meadow near what is now known as Slaughter Bridge – though it seems to have been so called only since the mid-eighteenth century. The name was formerly applied to the ancient granite monolith, some 3 metres long, with an almost totally illegible Latin inscription, which now lies on the river bank 180 metres north of the bridge, and which was used as a footbridge on Lord Falmouth's estate at Worthy Vale. If Slaughter Bridge is a genuinely ancient name it probably derives, like other 'Slaughter' place-names, from Old English words meaning 'mud' or 'blackthorn'. Nevertheless, Slaughter Bridge is nowadays an obviously suitable name for the site of the tragic battle which is likely enough really to have happened in the early sixth century somewhere in Britain, and in which the great leader was defeated and killed.

Geoffrey records impossibly huge armies but little other detail. Later writers, in true romance style, have the river choked with corpses and running with blood. The sixteenth-century antiquary John Leland was told locally that pieces of armour and similar evidence of battle were occasionally dug up by farmers. He describes how Arthur and Mordred met and fought hand-to-hand on the bridge, and how Arthur killed Mordred. In Geoffrey, Mordred is Arthur's nephew; in later accounts (Malory, for example) Mordred is Arthur's son, begotten in an unwittingly incestuous relationship before Arthur's marriage on his half-sister, as he later discovers her to be, Morgawse.

There is little difference between nephew and natural son in the imaginative structure of traditional literature, and the battle between father and son is an ancient motif (e.g. Saul and Jonathan, Sohrab and Rustum). This small bridge and country place, quiet but for Arthurian visitors, is the appropriate setting for a constant drama which may take place anywhere.

SX 109855   OS 200
1 mile N of Camelford, reached by an unclassified road turning N off the A39

Roche Rock

The stark granite outcrop of Roche Rock forces itself up in a field by
the village of Roche; on this startling protuberance is perched a
fifteenth-century chapel, now in ruins. Such strange sites were often
chosen by recluses for their hermitage retreats, as if they were on the
borders of the natural and the supernatural just as they are on those of
earth and sky or sea. There could have been a much earlier hermitage
here. E. M. R. Ditmas, in *Tristan and Iseult in Cornwall* (Gloucester:
Forrester Roberts, 1969), argues that this must have been the site of the
dwelling of the hermit Ogrin, where Tristan and Iseult took shelter in
their flight from the court of King Mark.

SW 991596   OS 200
Roche village is 7 miles NW of St Austell on the B3274, just S of the A30

St Dennis' Churchyard

This church and churchyard are on the site of an ancient fortress on the steep hill north of the town of St Dennis, and make an excellent viewpoint for the surrounding countryside. Domesday Book (1086) names a manor in the parish, 'Dimelihoc', which Geoffrey Ashe identifies with the 'Dimilioc' where, according to Geoffrey of Monmouth, Gorlois (the first husband of Ygerna, mother of Arthur) was killed.

The walls of the churchyard follow the lines of the inner rampart of the Iron Age fortification, giving it an unusual circular shape; but most of the present church is fifteenth century. To the north can be seen Castle-an-Dinas, the other candidate for the 'Dimilioc' where Gorlois was besieged (see TINTAGEL).

SW 951583   OS 200
St Dennis is midway between St Austell and Newquay, reached by turning E off the B3279

Zennor

An Arthurian story which appears not to occur elsewhere is associated with Zennor, between St Ives and Land's End. When red-headed Danes landed in Whitesand Bay near Sennen, to the north of Land's End, Arthur came to the rescue, and at the junction of the townships of Zennor, Gulval and Madron he dined with four Cornish kings on a large flat stone, Zennor Quoit, while the British forces were gathering to attack the Danes – whom they successfully routed. The Danes had stayed so long that birds had nested in the rigging of their ships and they had begotten many red-haired children on the local girls. Zennor Quoit is the capstone, now tipped on end, of an unopened megalithic burial-chamber, consisting of five upright stones and two vertical slabs of the façade of an antechamber. Red-haired children as bastards are the subject of other comic folktales in Europe, but it is curious to find this one attaching itself, though indirectly, to Arthur and the dining of the kings at the stone, though outstanding stories themselves attract other stories. The legend shows the general availability of Arthur as saviour folk-hero.

The Church of St Senara was given to Tywardreath Priory, one of Cornwall's chief monastic houses, in 1150, and partly dates from that time. One of the bench-ends, now part of a chancel seat, is carved with the Mermaid of Zennor; and the rather grim aspect of the church conveys something of its rugged surroundings, seldom hospitable to the foreign invader.

SW 454385   OS 203
5 miles SW of St Ives, between St Ives and St Just, on the B3306; Zennor Quoit is 1 mile SE of the village, approached by a footpath from the B3306

Trereen Dinas

Trereen Dinas, another Iron Age hillfort, is situated on the great promontory called Gurnard's Head; it has attracted Arthurian associations from its dramatic position, and claims to have been one of the castles used by Arthur in his campaign against the Danes (see ZENNOR). It does not have the further historical interest of TINTAGEL, but it demonstrates again the fondness of the popular imagination for humanising striking natural scenery.

SW 432387   OS 203
On Gurnard's Head, midway between St Ives and St Just, reached by a path turning N off the B3306 at Gurnard's Head Hotel

Whitesand Bay
(overleaf)

Here are said to have landed those red-headed Danes whom Arthur drove off, after their somewhat protracted stay (see ZENNOR). It is a good place to land, since the coastal cliffs here give way to the white sands which give the bay its name.

SW 360270   OS 203
2 miles N of Land's End, reached by an unclassified road turning NW off the A30

St Levan's Stone

This strikingly cleft rock is in St Levan's churchyard. St Levan was yet another of those exported Irish saints with whom Cornwall seems almost to have been crowded in the fifth and sixth centuries. Several stories were told about him, and the ancient cleft stone in the churchyard was apparently an object of veneration in Arthurian times. Later folktale recounts that Arthur and Merlin visited it. Further embroidery has Merlin or Levan split the stone, and an English jingle says that when pack-horses can pass through it 'the world will be done'.

SW 380222   OS 203
Near the coast, 4 miles SE of Land's End, reached by an unclassified road turning S off the B3315

St Michael's Mount
(overleaf)

A striking and romantic scene attracts a story. St Michael's Mount, so called since the time of Domesday Book (1086), was presumably named after the larger but very similar tidal island off the coast of France, Mont-Saint-Michel, by the monks from the great abbey there who colonised the Cornish island. (It was at the French Mont-Saint-Michel that King Arthur, according to Geoffrey of Monmouth, killed a loathsome giant, an episode that filters through to the English alliterative *Morte Arthure* and from there to Malory.)

The Arthurian associations of St Michael's Mount derive from the inventiveness and knowledge of Cornwall of the late-twelfth-century Anglo-Norman poet Beroul. In his version of the story of Tristan the effect of the love-potion on Tristan and Iseult wears off after their idyllic sojourn in the forest, and Iseult wishes to return to her husband, King Mark; but she has, as ladies say, 'nothing to wear' to suit so important an occasion. Her host, the hermit Ogrin, therefore goes to the fair at St Michael's Mount to buy her a second trousseau, as it were, for the reconciliation. There probably was a market here in the twelfth century, though the invention of romancers does not depend much on material fact.

SW 514298   OS 203
In Mount's Bay, near Marazion, 3 miles E of Penzance

Looe Pool

Looe Pool, the largest 'lake' (or, rather, lagoon) in Cornwall, in its beautiful situation between land and ocean, is a suitable place to imagine that final gesture relinquishing life, the casting away of Arthur's magic sword Excalibur, image of his charismatic power, and his departure to a mysterious otherworld.

The story of Excalibur was developed by French authors in the thirteenth century, whence it came to Malory, who tells it most movingly, and so to Tennyson. Sir Bedivere, a solitary survivor attendant on Arthur after the fatal battle (which Malory locates on Salisbury Plain, not at 'Camlann' – see SLAUGHTER BRIDGE), twice deceives Arthur and only pretends to have obeyed his command to throw away the sword. But Arthur is aware of this, and makes him go a third time and really cast it away. Tennyson may have known Looe Pool, for he describes in *The Passing of Arthur* how Bedivere carried the wounded king to a chapel

> That stood on a dark strait of barren land:
> On one side lay the Ocean, and on one
> Lay a great water, and the moon was full.

At the king's first command, Bedivere

> By zigzag paths and juts of pointed rock
> Came on the shining levels of the lake . . .

but hid the precious sword among the bulrushes on the edge. At the king's second command, he went

> Across the ridge and paced beside the mere
> Counting the dewy pebbles, fix'd in thought.

The third time he leapt lightly down the ridges and hurled in the sword;

> But ere he dipt the surface, rose an arm
> Clothed in white samite, mystic, wonderful,
> And caught him by the hilt, and brandish'd him
> Three times, and drew him under in the mere.

Then comes the boat with the lamenting queens who carry Arthur to the vale of Avalon to be healed of his wounds.

SW 645248   OS 203
An inlet of Mount's Bay, 2 miles SW of Helston

Tristan's Stone

This starkly impressive mono-lith near Fowey may well date from the sixth century, though it has been moved several times and its original position is unknown. It has an inscription in Latin, now virtu-ally illegible, to the effect that Drustanus, son of Cunomorus, lies here. 'Drustanus' is the Latinised form of 'Tristan' (itself modernised from the original Welsh), and 'Cunomorus' is that of 'Cynvawr', the name of a king who ruled in this part of Britain in the sixth century and who was otherwise known as Mark. If the 'Drustanus' of the stone is iden-tified with 'our' Tristan, then the tale could be interpreted as a version of the Oedipus situation, in which a man falls in love with his father's wife. However that may be, Celtic shadows lie thick about this area. (See also St Sampson's Church.)

SX 112522 OS 204
1 mile NW of Fowey on the A3082

St Sampson's Church

St Sampson's Church is beautifully situated above the River Fowey, with the small village of Golant below. Celtic origins being strong here, it is not surprising that the area became associated with the story of Tristan and Iseult.

St Sampson appears to have had a contemporary of the same name, described by Geoffrey of Monmouth as Archbishop of York, and the records of the two men's lives are confused. 'Our' Sampson seems to have been a Welshman who was born about 500 in what was Glamorgan (now Gwent) and became a student of St Ultyd at Llantwit Major in South Wales. He was a fiery missionary zealot who travelled to Ireland, worked here in Cornwall, and finished his career as Bishop of Dol in Brittany, returning perhaps to Wales to die soon after 557. The parish of Golant became so identified with St Sampson as to take over his name. This unusual treatment of a church dedication, together with various legends attaching Sampson to the district, suggests that he may really have stayed here in his lifetime, which coincided with 'Arthurian' times. He is part of that stream of travellers between Wales and Ireland, Cornwall and Brittany which was responsible for the spread of so many Arthurian stories – or of stories later drawn into the Arthurian orbit, like that of Tristan and Iseult.

Tristan is closely associated with this area, for there is TRISTAN'S STONE near Fowey, and the hillfort of Castle Dore just above St Sampson's Church is associated with King Mark. The first literary reference is by the Anglo-Norman romancer Beroul, who in his poem 'The Romance of Tristan' (written about 1190) tells an early version of the Tristan story. Either he or his source seems to have known something of Cornish geography. According to Beroul, after Iseult eloped with Tristan to live

with him in the forest, she was reconciled with King Mark in St Sampson's Church, described as a monastery of cathedral-like splendour. Beroul may have thought of the Iron Age camp at Castle Dore as the site of Mark's castle and court. The present St Sampson's Church dates from the early sixteenth century (and contains some fine wood carving); but we walk on Arthurian or Tristanian ground around these parts.

SX 121552   OS 200
3 miles N of Fowey, above the village of Golant, reached by turning E off the B3269

Dozmary Pool

Remote pools attract the imagination. They are images of the unknown, the lost, and the dreary, but also of potential recovery – a source of mystery. Dozmary Pool on Bodmin Moor is 275 metres above sea level, and is sufficiently remote and desolate to make it a fitting place for the final reception of Excalibur and the passing of Arthur (see Looe Pool).

SX 195745   OS 201
13 miles NE of Bodmin, reached by an unclassified road turning SE off the A30 at Bolventor

Trethevy Quoit

Trethevy Quoit is one of a considerable number of great stones (Geoffrey Ashe counts eleven) which have come to be called locally 'Arthur's Quoit'. A quoit is defined by *The Concise Oxford Dictionary* as a 'heavy flattish sharp-edged iron ring thrown to encircle iron peg or to fix it in ground near it in game of quoits'. To call these colossal stones 'quoits' is a jesting metaphor which imagines Arthur as a giant and the stones as his playthings, and draws on the depths of that folk-mind which we all share. Arthur's Quoit at Trethevy, as in other cases, is really the roughly rounded capstone of a megalithic burial-chamber, which was walled with other great stones. Formerly the chamber contained corpses splendidly buried, and the whole was covered by a mound of earth, but weathering, or sometimes human interference, has removed the earth covering, leaving the stones gaunt to the sky: empty chambers, mysteriously created, retaining some numinous power for the historically imaginative beholder. What better figure to see as originally casting these stones here than Arthur, 'the sleeping Lord'? This is not the chivalric Arthur, certainly, but a vague grand presence, with some humour and playfulness, active in the depths of our minds, yet leaving his mark on the land itself.

SX 259688   OS 201
3 miles N of Liskeard, between St Clear and Darite, near the village of Tremar, N of the B3254

Blackingstone Rock
(overleaf)

Only the Devil, say folklorists, is more often mentioned in local legend than Arthur. There are not many associations of Arthur with Devon, but here local legend has it that he met and fought with the Devil. The story illustrates the imaginative response to a striking natural feature. The crag erupts dramatically out of the hillside and has a great cleft in it. It is marked by ancient stresses and millennia of conflict with the weather. Like a boundary between man and primeval nature, it is a fitting place for a struggle between king and Devil.

SX 786856   OS 191
11 miles SW of Exeter, reached by an unclassified road turning SE off the B3213 2 miles E of Moretonhampstead

South and South-East Britain

Of several competing theories about Arthur, one of the most plausible sees him as a Briton chieftain who resisted the English drive across the southern part of Britain. His victorious battle at Mount Badon has been located at places with the element *Bad-* in their name, such as Badbury Rings in Dorset (*Introduction*, p. 22).

Even more notable is GLASTONBURY, rich in history and historical legend, where there has been a determined attempt to locate Arthur ever since the twelfth century, and where it was claimed that his grave was discovered in 1190 or 1191 (*Introduction*, p. 18). There, it was thought, he had been taken, mortally wounded from the last battle at Camlann. For long Glastonbury has been claimed as Avalon, and certainly the aura of an ancient sacred place, with hill and spring and a sequence of churches, is still to be felt despite all the modern clutter.

While Arthur is supposed to have died at Glastonbury, it has often been held that his court of Camelot was located on or around the hill at South Cadbury, where the fortifications, known now as CADBURY CASTLE, were extensively excavated in the 1970s by Leslie Alcock. The settlement was inhabited for many centuries, and some fifth- or sixth-century chieftain, successor of Iron Age and Roman occupiers, may well have held his court there, if not with chivalric trappings. Nearby is a river Cam, with villages called QUEEN CAMEL and West Camel. Both Leland and Camden record the local belief that Arthur's palace was here.

By contrast, Camelot is firmly located by Sir Thomas Malory at WINCHESTER, the capital of King Alfred's Wessex in the ninth century. What is remarkably Arthurian about Winchester now is the ROUND TABLE, hung in the Great Hall, and scientifically dated to the fourteenth century, though painted with its present design by order of Henry VIII in the sixteenth century.

The most remarkable monument in England is on the line down to the south-west: STONEHENGE. So outstanding a feature could not avoid being associated with Britain's hero, and Geoffrey of Monmouth has Merlin bringing the stones in from Ireland. Not far from Stonehenge is AMESBURY CHURCH, which later writers turned into an abbey to which Guinevere withdrew in penitence after Arthur's death.

There have been attempts to locate some of the historical Arthur's battles at ILCHESTER, LANGPORT and PORTCHESTER. Malory, with his interest in the eastern side of England and his strong sense of the practicalities of a period he considered to be very like his own, firmly identifies Dover as the place where people land from France, and consequently the natural place for Arthur and Gawain to land with their army to attack the traitor Mordred. Gawain was killed in the assault, and according to Malory his body was buried in DOVER CASTLE. Caxton even asserts in his 1485 edition of Malory's *Le Morte Darthur* that Gawain's skull is still to be seen in Dover Castle, along with 'Cradock's mantle'. As this last is certainly pure fantasy, one wonders how serious Caxton was about Arthur.

London has always been important since Roman times, and there is little doubt that an historical Arthur would have known of it, or perhaps knew it. But the scarcity of authentic ancient legends is inevitable, given the extensive development in later times of the south-eastern part of England, and the heavy pressure exerted there by the English since their earliest advent in the fifth century. Besides, until comparatively recent times much of East Anglia was cut off by the Fens, and during the ninth and tenth centuries England east of Watling Street (now the A5) was the Danelaw, under Danish control. Celtic legend was therefore least likely to flourish in that area.

The most magical parts of the south are Stonehenge in Salisbury Plain, and Glastonbury in Somerset, 'the summer country'. The attraction of Stonehenge is strangely illustrated by the increasingly large pop festivals held there in the early 1980s until they were forbidden in 1985, though regrettably Stonehenge itself now has to be defended by a barbed-wire fence.

Glastonbury remains the supreme Arthurian site, with its accretion of history and legend – from the original lake-dwellers to the Celts and their peripatetic saints, the Arthurian images of Avalon, and the series of churches. The modern writer J. C. Powys had a mystical sense of the supernatural powers which he felt were focussed on Glastonbury. In *A Glastonbury Romance* (1932), Powys' great achievement was to translate that intuition into characters and a story which are fully modern. In particular he invokes the story of the Holy Grail, while the central character, Mr Geard, is in some respects a modern Merlin. There are many other partial and fleeting identifications with Arthurian story, modern reincarnations of past characters and events. Present-day celebrations at Glastonbury continue this strange sense of the forces which created the ancient stories. Powys sees life as 'war-to-the-death' between the spirits of Good and Evil. These spirits exist in our consciousness, which is itself part of our bodies, and our bodies move on the land and are part of the same material substance as the earth. For such as Powys the very land has a kind of consciousness. He also felt the analogy between the historical Arthur's time and our own. In the preface to his other Arthurian novel, *Porius* (1951), set in the Dark Ages, and not so localised as *A Glastonbury Romance*, Powys writes:

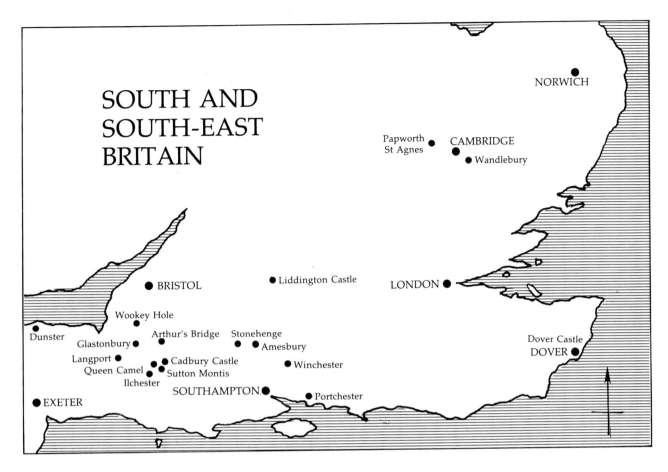

SOUTH AND
SOUTH-EAST
BRITAIN

NORWICH

Papworth
St Agnes ● ● CAMBRIDGE
● Wandlebury

● Liddington Castle

BRISTOL ●

LONDON ●

Wookey Hole
●

Dunster
●

Arthur's Bridge
Glastonbury ● ● Stonehenge
● ● Amesbury

Dover Castle
DOVER ●

Langport ●
Queen Camel ● ● Cadbury Castle
● Sutton Montis
Ilchester

● Winchester

SOUTHAMPTON ●

● Portchester

● EXETER

As we contemplate this historic background to the autumn of the last year of the fifth century, it is impossible not to think of the background of human life from which today we watch the first half of the twentieth century dissolve into its second half. As the old gods were departing then, so the old gods are departing now.

Glastonbury in the fifth century, with Arthur as a great king, has also been re-created in a more traditional way in other Arthurian novels of the latter part of the twentieth century. The trilogy by Mary Stewart, *The Crystal Cave* (1970), *The Hollow Hills* (1973), and *The Last Enchantment* (1979), is especially enjoyable, and the first two titles show her awareness of the importance of the land to the legend.

Some modern tales of Arthur have moved the focus somewhat from the hero–king to Merlin and magic. In this respect they have returned to something like the ancient attitude of folktale and legend, where Arthur is not always venerated, and there is a strong sense of myth and magic, rooted in the land itself.

Dunster Castle

Dunster in Somerset has had a castle since before the Norman Conquest. It is still a magnificent sight, though its earliest portion is now the thirteenth-century gateway, and it dominates the town. It is perhaps on the site of the citadel Dindraitho, which appears in the eleventh- or twelfth-century Life of St Carannog, one of the many Welsh saints who descended upon the south-west part of Britain. He left Cardigan and, when he came to the Bristol Channel, launched an altar onto the sea in order to find out where he should go to preach. It came to the realm of Cato and Arthur, who are said to have held court at Dindraitho. Carannog, seeking his altar, met Arthur, who promised to tell him where it was if Carannog would rid him of a dangerous serpent. Such was the saint's power that the serpent came running to him making a great noise, like a calf to its mother, and Carannog led it about, using his stole as a leash round its neck, before sending it off with orders to do no more harm. Arthur in return gave back Carannog's altar, which he had tried unsuccessfully to use as a table – it had thrown off everything put on it. Arthur also gave Carannog land on which he built churches at 'Carrum' and 'Carrov'. The general area is between the Quantocks and Exmoor, where Dunster lies. 'Carrum' may be nearby Carhampton; 'Carrov' may be Doniford.

SS 991435   OS 181
3 miles SE of Minehead, just off the A396

Glastonbury

Glastonbury is one of the most ancient inhabited holy places in Britain. Nowhere is better suited for some association with Arthur. The first inhabitants were Celts, living in what is now meadowland and orchards but was then a large lake. They occupied a village of houses of wattle-and-daub perched above the water on posts, and were probably massacred by a second invasion of Celts in the first century. The lake slowly dwindled to marshes and pools, watered by the River Brue, but Glastonbury is still something of an island. The sharp conical hill on the island is still known by the Celtic name of *Tor*. A spring, Chalice Well, is nearby. (See pp. 64–5 below.) The high ground by a spring on an island has been a sacred place from pagan times. Glastonbury Tor became Christian perhaps as early as the second century, and there was an ancient cemetery, perhaps pre-Christian, where the earliest of a series of churches was built, in the area of what is now the Lady Chapel of the abbey. Many Irish and Welsh saints visited Glastonbury, and St Patrick, the Welshman who converted the Irish to Christianity in the fifth century, is said to have been buried here in 463.

It is small wonder that this sacred place came to be thought of as Avalon in the twelfth century, by Geoffrey of Monmouth and others. They connected the word with the Welsh *aval* ('apple'); perhaps Somerset was then, as now, a notable place for apple growing. Apples, that most common fruit, have always had a magical aura; they grow in the garden of Hesperides, which is a sort of classical Earthly Paradise, and Geoffrey of Monmouth also refers to *Insula Pomorum* ('the Island of Apples') as the place to which the poet and wizard Taliesin took the wounded Arthur at the end of his life. Apples are symbols of joy and healing. Some of us still say 'An apple a day keeps the doctor away'. Symbols of power are often ambiguous. Classical legend also has an apple of discord, and popular legend, though not the Bible itself, has it that the fruit with which the Serpent tempted Eve, and Eve Adam, was an apple. Avalon is a place of death as well as of healing.

Avalon was also thought to be named after a British king Avalloc, who dwelt there with his daughters, including Morgan the enchantress.

Why was Glastonbury thought to be Avalon? In the twelfth century some of the Welsh called Glastonbury 'glass island', and in Welsh mythology 'glass island' was one of the ways of imagining the Otherworld. The wateriness of the surroundings of Glastonbury – a landscape still criss-crossed by hundreds of little dykes – may have helped.

Christianity came early to Glastonbury. Legend says that Joseph of Arimathea came with eleven companions bringing either the chalice of the Last Supper, or the phials which held Christ's blood caught in the chalice. The oldest certain Christian church was probably built about 166, and a series of increasingly large churches followed. The great St Dunstan (died 988) was abbot, and Saxon kings were buried here. In 1184 the whole abbey was burned down and building was begun on a splendid new church, not completed until 1303. The first part to be finished was the Lady Chapel, on the very site of the most ancient of the former churches. The abbey was destroyed during the Reformation, in 1539, and now its ruins hauntingly evoke its former glory. Our pictures show the two great piers at the junction of the nave and chancel, and (overleaf) details of the carving in the Lady Chapel.

The discovery of Arthur's grave in 1190 or 1191 has been discussed above (*Introduction*, p. 18). Giraldus Cambrensis, 'Gerald the Welshman', writing the first chapter of his *De Principis Instructione* ('Of the Education of a Prince') between 1193 and 1199, says that the grave was between two stone pyramids in the churchyard at Glastonbury (its site is now carefully marked by the Department of the Environment) and that the body was buried deep in the ground in a hollowed oak. A leaden cross was fixed to a stone beneath the coffin, inscribed in Latin: 'Here lies buried the famous king Arthur with Guinevere his second wife in the island of Avalon.' Two-thirds of the coffin had the bones of a huge man, the other third those of a woman. A lock of woman's hair, fresh and golden, was picked out, only to fall immediately to dust. The king's bones showed ten wounds, the last unhealed. The remains were eventually reburied in front of the high altar.

Even this did not dispel the legend of Arthur's return. It only confirmed his greatness and the claims of Glastonbury as an Arthurian centre and place of pilgrimage (especially today). It did not even stop other places being called Avalon.

Glastonbury never claimed to be Arthur's dwelling-place, only his burial-place. The Life of St Gildas written by Caradoc of Llancarfan in the twelfth century says that Melvas, king of 'the summer region' (Somerset?), carried off Guinevere and held her captive at Glastonbury for a year. This is obviously a version of the capture of a queen by the King of the Otherworld, as found in classical and Celtic legend. It is a sort of death myth. The story becomes progressively more 'realistic' until in Malory's fifteenth-century version in *Le Morte Darthur* the queen is carried off by Meleagaunt, a disaffected knight and disappointed lover, to his castle not far from Lambeth in London. In Malory's story the rescuer is Lancelot, but in the Life of St Gildas Arthur himself searches for her with an

army. War between the two kings is avoided, and Guinevere's return obtained, by the mediation of St Gildas. Arthur and Melvas endow the abbey richly.

Malory writes of the wounded Arthur's passing into the care of ladies who came in a boat, 'and among them all was a queen, and all they had black hoods' (see LOOE POOL). They rowed away, leaving the faithful Bedivere desolate. 'What shall become of me?' he cried. 'Comfort thyself,' said the king, 'and do as thou mayst, for in me is no trust for to trust in. For I must into the vale of Avalon to heal me of my grievous wound. And if thou hear nevermore of me, pray for my soul!'

The next day Bedivere found a mysterious grave in a chapel between two grey woods, near to Glastonbury, and a hermit mourning, and deduced that it was the grave of Arthur. Malory adds that he could find no more of 'the very certainty of his death' for the hermit did not know for certain that the buried corpse was that of Arthur, and some men say Arthur shall come again. Malory comes to no conclusion but that 'here in this world he changed his life'.

Queen Guinevere withdrew to AMESBURY, but Malory tells how she was buried at Glastonbury and how Lancelot swooned upon her tomb. When reproached for making such sorrow, he replied that it was not 'for any rejoicing of sin, but my sorrow may never have end. For when I remember of her beauty and of her noblesse, that was both with her king and with her, so when I saw his corpse and her corpse so lie together, truly my heart would not serve to sustain my careful body.'

This is a late literary treatment. Much earlier and simpler tales, likewise concerned with death, are also associated with Glastonbury. For example, there is one which relates that Arthur was keeping Christmas at Caerleon and knighted a youth called Ider. Arthur took Ider with him to fight three giants. Ider went ahead and slew them but died himself. Arthur, reproaching himself for his slowness in coming to the support of Ider, established twenty-four monks at Glastonbury and endowed them richly.

Equally strange, but far richer in content, is the most famous of all stories about Glastonbury, the modern novel by John Cowper Powys, *A Glastonbury Romance* (1932). In the 1955 edition the author stated that his purpose was 'to convey a jumbled-up and squeezed together epitome of life's various dimensions'. Impossible to summarise, with over fifty characters, the complex story is realistic, supernatural, pagan, Christian, satirical, comical. The main setting is Glastonbury, which, the author maintains, has the largest residue of unused magical power in the world.

The story of Joseph of Arimathea became attached to Glastonbury, and hence to Arthurian legend, through the association of the Round Table with the Quest for the Holy Grail. Joseph of Arimathea, according to Luke XXIII, took down the body of Jesus from the Cross and laid it in a rock-hewn tomb. Legend has it that he caught the blood from Christ's pierced side in the chalice used for the Last Supper, and carefully preserved it. Some later storytellers identified the chalice with the Holy Grail which came to Arthur's court, signifying Christian joy and plenty, but also bringing about the end of Arthur's earthly glory.

St Joseph was said to have come to England to preach the gospel. He laboured up Wearyall (Wyrral) Hill near Glastonbury and struck his staff into the ground. There it sprouted leaves and flowers, becoming the Glastonbury Thorn, which flowered on Christmas Day. The Puritans hacked it down, but offshoots were planted in the abbey grounds and are said to retain the power to bloom on Christmas Day.

ST 501390   OS 182
26 miles SW of Bath, reached by the A39 or the A361

Chalice Well

The Grail legend has drawn Chalice Well into its magic circle. Wells by hills, especially by so striking a hill as Glastonbury Tor, often have magical or supernatural healing powers attributed to them, and this attribution may be very ancient in the case of Chalice Well. It is a 'red' well, tinctured by chalybeate, and was sometimes called 'Blood Spring'. 'Chalice Well' is a corruption of the earlier *Chalcwelle* ('Chalk Well'); the change came in medieval times, caused by the popularity of the Grail legends since the thirteenth century. Water and blood from Christ's side were caught in a chalice by St Joseph; now the sacred earth itself 'bleeds'.

ST 508386   OS 182
The entrance to Chalice Well Garden is on the A361 to Shepton Mallet

Glastonbury Tor

Glastonbury Tor was probably from ancient times a sacred place, as many hilltops are throughout the world, in many cultures. The tower which now surmounts it is all that remains of the Church of St Michael, which was built in the fourteenth century, replacing an earlier church. Remnants of a sixth-century settlement have been found on the side of the Tor – perhaps the abode of a 'real' Melvas, or even of Arthur?

ST 512386   OS 182
On the outskirts of Glastonbury, reached by Well House Lane, a turning N off the A361

Langport Church

The fine fifteenth-century church at Langport has some excellent glass, including, in the lower right panel of the east window (shown here), a picture of Joseph of Arimathea (see GLASTONBURY). Joseph is carrying what appear to be two holy vessels, containing, it is thought, the blood and the sweat of Christ. Some have wished to see Langport as Llongborth, which an early Welsh poem in the Black Book of Carmarthen names as the place of the battle at which the leader Gerrans, or Geraint, was killed and 'Arthur's brave men' were hewn with steel. Gerrans or Geraint may have been Gerontius, the last independent Celtic king of the south-western kingdom of Dumnonia, but wherever Llongborth was there is no reason to think it was Langport in Somerset; and anyway Gerontius was killed by the English King Ina of Wessex in 710. Langport is a quite common English place-name, probably meaning 'long market-place', according to *The Oxford Dictionary of English Place-Names.*

ST 422267   OS 193
14 miles E of Taunton, on the A378

The River at Ilchester

Ilchester was a town of some importance both in Romano-British and in medieval times. Its Celtic name was Lindinis, which recalls Linnius, the name of the region in which, according to Nennius, Arthur fought four battles on the River Dubglas. The River Yeo, shown here, flows past Ilchester before bending south to Yeovil. At Ilchester fragments have been found of the same kind of fifth-century pottery as is found at TINTAGEL, and CADBURY is not far away, so that it is easy to think of Ilchester as part of the Arthurian scene.

ST 521226   OS 183
6 miles N of Yeovil, on the B3151

River Cam at Queen Camel

The River Cam flows near CADBURY CASTLE. If Arthur ruled at Cadbury Castle and the battle of Camlann took place somewhere near, then the River Cam may be the water along which the wounded Arthur was carried to Avalon (GLASTONBURY). There is a local tradition of many graves found in a field between the river and Cadbury Castle, indicating an ancient battle. Both the river-name Cam ('crooked') and the place-name Camel ('long ridge') are Celtic. The village Queen Camel is so called because Edward I gave it to his queen, Eleanor, in the late thirteenth century, but the 'British' (that is, Celtic) roots are strong.

ST 598250   OS 183
6 miles N of Yeovil, the river runs under the A359 at Queen Camel

Sutton Montis Church

On Christmas Eve, so it is said, Arthur and his men come down from the hollow hill of CADBURY CASTLE to drink from a well by the church of Sutton Montis. The well, in the orchard of Abbey House, is now bricked over but can be clearly seen from the north wall of the churchyard. That any imaginable Arthur should come so far to drink *water* seems a strange fancy, but in medieval times the eve of a feast was a fast, so the tale is perhaps appropriate, and may be relatively ancient. Ancient heroes are often thought to live on in hollow hills.

The church at Sutton Montis dates back in large part to the thirteenth century, though the nave was rebuilt in 1805. Instead of the usual church porch it has, on the south side, a charmingly incongruous structure on Tuscan columns which looks as if it ought to belong to a small manor house.

ST 624248   OS 183
6 miles S of Wincanton, just S of the A303

Cadbury Castle

Cadbury Castle is an Iron Age fortified settlement which has acquired Arthurian associations. It is very extensive, some 20 acres in area, and has a series of earthen ramparts surrounding the top, from which there is a magnificent view, including GLASTONBURY TOR to the north-west, 12 miles away. The site was intermittently occupied long before the sixth century, and there seems to have been a substantial sixth-century settlement. Now it is a pleasingly rustic space of rough ground, much of it wooded, but it is possible to walk round the lower ramparts of the first wall.

The antiquary Leland, in 1542, seems to have been the first to call Cadbury Castle Camelot, and in this he was followed by Camden. Leland vouches for local legend that it was Arthur's stronghold and that Roman coins and a silver horseshoe had been found there. Camden tells us that the local people called it Arthur's palace. 'Folks say', or said according to stories collected about 1890, that on the night of the full moon King Arthur and his men ride round the hill; their horses are shod with silver, and they water them at the Wishing Well. The well, in the lowest rampart, is known as King Arthur's Well. An ancient trackway going towards Glastonbury is called Arthur's Lane or Causeway.

The hill has been believed by some to be hollow. There are gates in it (though no one has seen them recently) either of iron or of gold, through which, on St John's Eve (23 June, the eve of Midsummer Day), a king may be seen sitting with his court. It was here, some time in the 1890s, that an old man asked a party of antiquarian searchers if they had come to take the king away. The folk-memory of Arthur lives on.

ST 628252   OS 183
5 miles SW of Wincanton, reached from the village of South Cadbury, just off the A303

Wookey Hole

It is hard for any striking natural feature in Britain not to be associated with either Arthur or the Devil. The great underground caves formed by the River Axe, deep in the Mendip Hills, have been occupied by human beings, on and off, for at least two thousand years. An evil witch was once thought to dwell in the caves and is mentioned by the chronicler William of Worcester, who visited the caves in 1470. The caves are the most splendid thing of their kind in Britain and well worth a visit; but only their atmospheric power can have prompted the fantasy that the witch was the Black Hag whose blood Arthur seeks in the ancient Welsh tale of 'Culhwch and Olwen' in *The Mabinogion*.

The entrance to the caves is through the spectacular ravine shown in our picture, where the River Axe emerges from under the hills; caves in the ravine show traces of animal and human life in Palaeolithic times, 50,000 years ago.

ST 531480   OS 182
2 miles NW of Wells, reached by unclassified roads turning N off the A371

Arthur's Bridge

Not even modern ingenuity can discover a reason why this little bridge over the gentle River Alham is so named, but it makes a pleasing picture.

ST 638358   OS 183
5 miles S of Shepton Mallet, a bridge over the River Alham on the A371

Stonehenge

(previous page)

This great stone circle on Salisbury Plain in Wiltshire is the grandest and the most ancient of British monuments, dating back perhaps as far as three thousand years. It inevitably provokes speculation and fantasy, the most fashionable theory today connecting it with Druids. There is no doubt that some at least of the stones were transported from the far-distant Prescelly Hills in west Wales, 200 miles away – a feat amazing in itself.

Geoffrey of Monmouth could not have known that, but he did better. According to him, King Aurelius, Arthur's uncle, wished to create a national monument to commemorate the British warriors killed by the Saxons (see AMESBURY CHURCH). He failed, so Merlin suggested bringing the Giants' Ring, a suitably grand cenotaph, from Ireland. Its stones had been brought from Africa, and had magical healing properties; but the Britons, having sent an army and defeated the Irish, were unable to move them. Merlin had to come to the rescue again with his magic arts and ship them over, at which point the Devil hit him on the heel with one of them – according to the antiquary John Aubrey, writing in 1686–7. As noted by Fairbairn and Cyprien, the heelprint is visible today on stone fourteen of the outer circle. Geoffrey mentions that Stonehenge is the circle's English name.

When Aurelius died he was buried at Stonehenge and was succeeded by his brother Uther, Arthur's father, who was also eventually buried there – as was Constantine, Arthur's successor.

SU 122422   OS 184
11 miles N of Salisbury, on Salisbury Plain; the entrance is on the A344 W of Amesbury

Amesbury Church

Geoffrey of Monmouth, following Nennius, tells how Hengist treacherously murdered 460 unarmed Britons who had come to a peace conference on Mount Ambrius. The dead were buried in the Cloister of Ambrius, near Salisbury. It was to commemorate these dead that the British king, Aurelius Ambrosius, obtained STONE-HENGE. The Cloister of Ambrius has been taken to be Amesbury, where the present abbey church is still partly twelfth century (that is, contemporary with Geoffrey) and replaces an earlier church, founded for Benedictine nuns in 980. The church was refounded as a priory in 1177, and by the early fourteenth century over a hundred nuns were living here; it was a favoured retreat for royal and noble ladies.

Somewhere in the creative evolution of Arthurian story (probably in a French romance) Guinevere was shown as retiring to the convent at

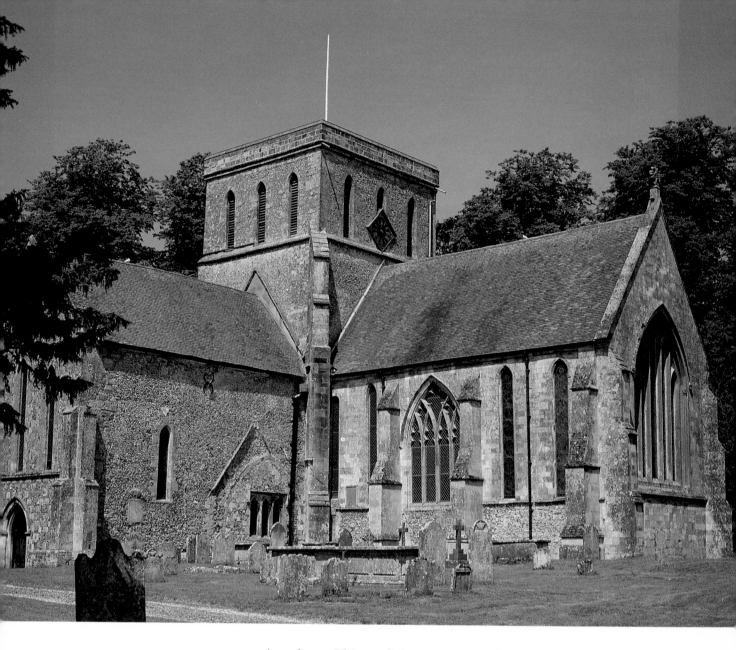

Amesbury. This tradition is preserved in the beautiful fourteenth-century English poem *Le Morte Arthur*, which in turn is followed by Malory, who gives the queen a most moving speech when, after Arthur's death, Lancelot visits her: 'Through this same man and me hath all this war been wrought, and the death of the most noblest knights of the world; for through our love that we have loved together is my most noble lord slain. Therefore, Sir Lancelot, wit thou well I am set in such a plight to get my soul's health.'

SU 150419   OS 184
8 miles N of Salisbury, on the A303 as it leaves Amesbury in the direction of Wincanton

Winchester Cathedral

Winchester was a Celtic, then a Roman, town. Later, in Anglo-Saxon times, under Alfred, it became the capital of Wessex and the chief English town. An English church was certainly begun in 643, and it was enlarged by the bishop, St Swithun himself, in 852–62; the present cathedral was begun in the eleventh century.

Under the crossing arch of the north transept is the Chapel of the Holy Sepulchre, inserted in about 1200. Its vault and walls were painted soon after with scenes from the life of Christ, including the Deposition from the Cross and the Entombment (shown overleaf) – perhaps the finest thirteenth-century wall paintings in Britain. The early-sixteenth-century reredos (shown opposite) carries nineteenth-century statues in its elaborately carved niches, expressive of the Victorian dream of medieval England.

SU 482293   OS 185
SE of the High Street in the centre of Winchester, which is 12 miles N of Southampton

The Round Table, Great Hall, Winchester
(overleaf)

The Great Hall at Winchester, part of the castle begun by William the Conqueror, is a superb example of thirteenth-century architecture. Above the remains of the royal dais hangs the great Round Table, thought to have been made in the thirteenth or fourteenth century. It was painted, or repainted, by order of Henry VIII, a great lover of Malory's work, in 1522, to mark the visit of the Emperor Charles V; at the centre is a Tudor rose. It was all repainted in 1729.

There are only twenty-five seats marked, the names of the knights being taken from Malory. When the Round Table is first mentioned in *Le Morte Darthur*, Malory describes it as having 150 seats, though at the end of the work, no doubt by Caxton's misprint, 140 is the number given. Casualness about precise numbers is in any case a mark of traditional literature and folktale.

The Round Table is first mentioned in the late twelfth century by the French poet Wace. In his versification of Geoffrey's *History* he tells how Arthur gathered many noble knights into his household. According to the Britons, says Wace, the Round Table was made so that each knight should be equal in status with the others, receiving equal service. No one could boast that he was higher than his fellow, and none was treated as an alien, though the knights came from many lands.

Later the 'Round Table' was used as a phrase to describe the whole fellowship of Arthur's knights, and in folklore the term sometimes describes a Roman amphitheatre or a natural circle of rocks.

SU 477293   OS 185
South of Westgate, at the west end of the High Street in the centre of Winchester

Portchester Castle

Portchester Castle has been claimed, like LANGPORT, as the site of the battle of Llongborth, in which Geraint was killed. The castle, situated on a low-lying promontory and surrounded on three sides by the sea, is on the site of a Roman fort, taken over first by the English and then by the Normans; it is one of the best Roman structures still to be seen in Britain. A visit is well worth while, for the castle is rich in historical evidence of the fusion of successive peoples in Britain to which the Arthurian stories bear witness.

The keep is on the site of the north-west angle of the Roman fort. Originally it had a basement, a tall main storey and high parapet walls which concealed the roof, but it was heightened in the twelfth century (probably before 1175). In the fourteenth century the castle was favoured as a royal residence.

SU 625045   OS 196
At the head of Portsmouth harbour, midway between Portsmouth and Fareham, reached from the A27

Dover Castle
(*overleaf*)

Dover Castle is splendidly sited on a hill overlooking the English Channel, commanding what came to be regarded in medieval times as the normal port of embarkation for and arrival from France. The castle picturesquely crowns the summit of the famous white cliffs, and in the Middle Ages was considered the key to England. There may have been an Iron Age fort; the octagonal *pharos*, possibly the oldest building in Britain, was built by the Romans in A.D. 50; later the English and then the Normans fortified the castle. The current building dates mainly from Norman times, though it was heavily restored in the nineteenth century.

A thirteenth-century French romance first brings Dover into Arthurian legend, and Malory perpetuates the tradition. The story concerns Mordred's attempt to seize power while Arthur is at war on the Continent. Arthur returns with Gawain, and makes an assault-landing at Dover against Mordred's army. Gawain is killed; 'and there the king made great sorrow out of measure, and took Sir Gawain in his arms, and thrice he there swooned . . . "Alas, Sir Gawain, my sister's son, here now thou liest, the man in the world that I loved most." ' The king has him buried in a chapel in Dover Castle, 'and there yet all men may see the skull of him'.

Caxton, in the Preface to his edition of Malory printed in 1485, says that 'in the castle of Dover ye may see Gawain's skull and Cradock's mantle'. Caxton was for thirty years a leading English merchant in Bruges and must surely have passed through Dover a number of times, so one would think he might be speaking from knowledge of these objects. However, 'Cradock's mantle' does not appear in Malory's *Le Morte Darthur*. The reference is to one Caradoc Briebras, in the thirteenth-century French romance called *Mantel Mautaille*. Caradoc's wife's chastity, along with that of all other ladies in Arthur's court, is tested by means of a magic mantle which will only fit chaste wives. Caradoc's wife is the only lady to pass the test. The theme is a favourite one in folktale. It appears in several romances and, as late as the seventeenth century, in an English ballad called *The Boy and the Mantle*, recorded in the Percy Folio, a manuscript of popular poetry.

TR 326418   OS 179
On the Kent coast, overlooking the town and harbour of Dover

Liddington Castle

The battle of Mount Badon has been the subject of fierce controversy – happily without the same slaughter, but also without the same success. Nennius, who wrote in Latin in the ninth century and was the earliest historian actually to mention Arthur, called it the king's twelfth battle (twelve is of course a 'magic' number). The battle is mentioned also by the sixth-century writer Gildas. Maybe it really was a successful attempt by the historical Arthur, or some British war-leader, to stem the advance of the invading English.

Places called Badbury are favoured by some enthusiasts for identifying Mount Badon. They include Badbury Rings in Dorset, Badbury in Wiltshire and a Badbury Hill in Oxfordshire (formerly in Berkshire). The name is also found as Badby and Baumber – there is plenty of choice. It is an Old English name, meaning 'Badda's burg' or fort, and these places are all near ancient earthworks. *The Oxford Dictionary of English Place-Names* suggests that Badda may have been a legendary hero associated with ancient strongholds.

One of these strongholds is Liddington Castle, a hillfort, presumably Iron Age, near the Wiltshire Badbury. It is close to a Roman road and the ancient Ridge Way across the Berkshire and Wiltshire downs. The strategic situation makes it a very likely place for the defeat of the westward-advancing English. Even in such a serene landscape it is easy to imagine the clash of arms and the slaughter around this ancient fortress, and to see it as a place of heroic achievement.

SU 208796   OS 174
1 mile S of junction 15 on the M4, reached by an unclassified road turning SW off the A419 Swindon–Hungerford road

The White Tower, London

London, on the Thames, was settled by the Celts and taken over by the Romans, who made it a substantial fortified town. It has always been an important commercial centre, and in the Middle Ages it was the only city in this island which came anywhere near the size and importance of the great Continental European cities. It comprised the area (about one square mile) still called 'the City', not to be confused with Westminster, which is a couple of miles upstream. London was a great port and trading centre, dominated by the Tower, while Westminster, with Abbey and Palace and Hall, was one of the chief sites of the royal court. London's great fortress, its importance as a trading centre and its closeness to royalty, caused it to be absorbed into Arthurian story early on.

There was some difficulty involved in this. Arthur originates in the archaic western and northern parts of the country, always on the defensive against the driving, modernising, dominant south-eastern part, which is nearest the Continent, and of which London is the supreme expression. London was therefore both attractive and dangerous, a magnet and a threat. It is both a centre and a margin for Arthurian story.

The earliest Welsh legend about London and Arthur, though very brief, illustrates this blend of remoteness and centrality. The legend occurs in the Triads in the Red Book of Hergest (*Introduction*, p. 8). It is twofold, concerning the 'Three Fortunate Concealments' of Britain, and the 'Three Unfortunate Disclosures'. These take us back to ancient roots, yet anyone who recognises the significance of London in World War II, with the weight of German attacks upon it, and the refusal of the king and government to leave it, will understand the subtlety and symbolic force of the apparently grotesque legend.

One of the 'Three Fortunate Concealments' was that of the head of Bran the Blessed, a son of King Lear unknown to Shakespeare. An eleventh-century poem, *Branwen*, records him as an early king of Britain who, like the Fisher King of the Grail legend, was wounded in battle. The Fisher King's wounded thigh suggests impaired virility; and in many ancient societies, from Wales to Japan, the virility of the king was closely associated with the fertility of the land. Bran's wound, too, led to the devastation of the land, though recovery followed. Before he was wounded Bran had associated with him a horn of plenty, in which appeared whatever food and drink was wished for by the fortunate possessor. Bran was beheaded, and there is a story of his retinue feasting in hall with his head on a dish. The head of Bran, according to the Triad, was buried in the White Hill in London, with its face towards France, and while it was there no foreign oppressor came to Britain.

One of the 'Three Unfortunate Disclosures' also concerns Bran's head, which Arthur had dug up, since he preferred that this island should be protected by no one's strength but his own. Attackers then came and ultimately prevailed.

This is the primitive Arthur of Celtic story, both heroic and recklessly proud. All such stories evoke a mixture of admiration, pride and sorrow. This one symbolises how the ancient magic of the tribe is abandoned for the risks of personal self-reliance, often tainted with pride. The fortunate concealment and unfortunate disclosure epitomise our superstitious longing for and belief in supernatural defence, while we do nothing. Their potency depends on our knowledge that in this island danger always comes from the east; that if we rely on ourselves we are open to human error; that modern weapons and strength (as opposed to ancient magic) may be defeated by better weapons and greater strength; and that even heroes die.

The White Hill in London, where Bran's head was buried, and where we wish it had been allowed to remain, is the site of the Tower of London, which thus enters Arthurian legend. The White Tower itself is the most ancient and grimly magnificent part of that great fortress which protected and dominated early London. Legend says that it was built by Julius Caesar; in fact it was begun soon after the Norman Conquest, but was completed in the twelfth century, to remain the key to London throughout the Middle Ages.

London's importance in the twelfth century was fully recognised by Geoffrey of Monmouth in his *History of the Kings of Britain*. He says that the capital of Britain was that great city on the Thames founded by Brutus, who conquered the island from giants, and after whom Britain was named. Brutus was the grandson of Aeneas, who, having been driven out of Troy, founded Rome. So Brutus, says Geoffrey (and his story was believed until the sixteenth century in Britain), named his capital *Troia Nova* ('New Troy'). Hence the mingled race of English, Celts and Normans, from the twelfth to the sixteenth century, believed themselves to be descendants of the Trojans, and they read the story of the fall of Troy with more sympathy for the losers than for the Greek victors. Troia Nova, says Geoffrey, became Trinovant. He had some feeling for Celtic origins; though he does not tell the story of Bran's head, he does tell how King Lud re-founded the city, renaming it Kaerlud ('the city of Lud'), which became Kaerlundein, and so London. (The City thoroughfare of Ludgate Hill is also named after this king.)

Geoffrey tells too how London was attacked by the Romans and eventually conquered by Julius Caesar, who exacted an annual tribute from the British to Rome. Arthur's father, King Utherpendragon, held court in London, and when Arthur as king was attacked by the English under Colgrim he retreated to London. But Geoffrey does not associate London or the White Tower with Arthur's nephew Mordred's rebellion and adultery with Guinevere, preferring, as he says, not to go into detail in these matters.

London emerges more prominently as Arthurian tales proliferate in French romances, and Malory gathers London-based events together with even greater emphasis and more precise locations. He obviously knew London and the neighbouring city of Westminster. In his account, King Utherpendragon's principal seat is at London, and it is at London's greatest church – whether St Paul's or not Malory cannot say – that the youthful Arthur proves himself the true king by being the only one who can draw the sword from the stone. Arthur also holds his first council in London, when menaced by many enemies. Presumably such councils took place in the Tower, but medieval kings' courts were always on the move, and Malory's Arthur also holds court at Camelot, 'which is Winchester', at Carlisle, and at Caerleon, where Arthur has himself crowned.

In the stories of *Le Morte Darthur* London plays generally a less than central part, but becomes more important in the progress towards final tragedy. It is in London that Queen Guinevere gives the private dinner-party at which a poisoned apple is introduced among the food. She is condemned for attempted murder, and this occasions the first of Lancelot's three great rescues of the queen. When Mordred betrays Arthur, he captures and intends to marry Guinevere ('which was his uncle's wife and his father's wife'), but, on the excuse of going to London to buy clothes and other necessities for the wedding, she escapes into the Tower and defends it against him. Mordred is well supported in his rebellion by men of the Home Counties and East Anglia; the east and south-east are the parts of England most hostile to Arthur.

The White Tower still stands, and from imprisonment in it many a good and great Englishman, as well as many a traitor, has gone to a grisly death on Tower Hill. But it kept Guinevere safe, and survives as an Arthurian stronghold in an ever more modern city.

TQ 336804   OS 176
On the River Thames NW of Tower Bridge

Wandlebury Ring

There are no well-grounded legends of Arthur in the Midlands or in the east of England, but a few traces of how the story crept across the country in late medieval times are of interest. The earliest example seems to be the University of Cambridge's mid-fifteenth-century claim to have been founded by King Arthur. The other examples (apart from London, which figures in Arthurian story from Geoffrey of Monmouth onwards) seem mostly to be due to Sir Thomas Malory, who imagined for the events he relates as convincing a setting as he could within the context of the fifteenth century. He (to some extent following the lead of French romances) is responsible for some references not only to London, but also to Dover (see THE WHITE TOWER and DOVER CASTLE) and to BAMBURGH and ALNWICK. More interesting is his reference to 'Wandesborow castle', which seems to be Wandlebury Ring, an Iron Age camp near Cambridge. If, as is usually assumed, he was the Sir Thomas Malory of Newbold Revel in Warwickshire, how should he know of this not very notable landmark, which has no other Arthurian association? It has been argued by R. R. Griffith – in *Aspects of Malory*, ed. T. Takamiya and Derek Brewer (Cambridge: D. S. Brewer, 1981) –that the author of *Le Morte Darthur* was in in fact a Thomas Malory who lived at Papworth St Agnes, a secluded village north-west of Cambridge. This would give an Arthurian association to the otherwise unlikely spot, and explain

Malory's knowledge of Wandlebury Ring. Our photographs show (above) part of the ditch in the Iron Age fortifications at Wandlebury, and (left) the present west front (dating from about 1700) of the Malory family's manor farm at Papworth St Agnes.

Wandlebury Ring
TL 494534   OS 154
3 miles SE of Cambridge on the A1307

Papworth St Agnes
TL 268645   OS 153
15 miles NW of Cambridge, reached by turning SW off the A14 5 miles S of
Huntingdon

Moel Arthur
(*opposite*)

Moel Arthur is a good example of how in Wales a striking natural and man-made feature, in this case an Iron Age hillfort 450 metres high arising out of flat surroundings, can attract the name of Arthur. It is a fine piece of countryside, but no surviving story attaches to it.

SJ 145660   OS 116
18 miles W of Chester between Denbigh and Mold, reached by an unclassified road turning SW off the A451

Hueil's Stone, Ruthin

(opposite)

A rough, and presumably very ancient, folktale found in early Welsh chronicles tells of rivalry and war between Arthur and a northern princeling, Hueil, said to be the elder brother of that Gildas whose writing begins the Arthurian record. The story is that Hueil tried to seduce one of Arthur's mistresses when Arthur was holding court at Caerwys, about 10 miles north of Ruthin. Arthur and Hueil fought. Arthur was wounded in the thigh and left with a limp. Hueil promised not to jeer at this sign of defeat, but later, when Arthur had gone to Ruthin to try to seduce another lady and went disguised in women's clothing to a dance to meet her, Hueil, who was there, commented on the clumsy dancing of the big 'woman'. Considering himself released from obligation to Hueil because of this remark, the enraged Arthur had Hueil beheaded on Maen Hueil, a piece of limestone now known as 'Hueil's Stone', in the market place by Exmewe Hall in Ruthin.

SJ 123583   OS 116
Ruthin is 18 miles NW of Wrexham

Caergai
(previous page)

The earthworks of a prehistoric fortress and traces of Roman walls in a seventeenth-century farmyard, on the top of a low hill overlooking Lake Bala from the south-west, have for long been called 'the fortress of Kei'. In 'The Dream of Rhonabwy' Kei and Bedwyr are Arthur's two closest and doughtiest companions. We are told that Kei could hold his breath for nine nights and days under water; he could go without sleep for nine nights; he could give a wound that would not heal; he could be as tall as the tallest tree in the forest. When it rained most heavily, the air a hand-breadth before his hand and another behind him would be dry, because of his great heat. He was represented as Arthur's seneschal, or steward, in later stories, which progressively blackened his character, until he became the deceitful, jealous, bitter-tongued knight whom Malory portrays. The fact that this particular spot in Merioneth is associated with Kei, however, suggests some ancient memory of his origins in Welsh story. Our picture looks south-eastward across the lake.

SH 877315   OS 125
4 miles SW of Bala, rising N of the A494 1 mile E of Llanwchllyn

Arthur's Rock, or Craig Arthur, Llangollen

A great ridge of rock runs north behind DINAS BRAN and ends in a striking cliff named after Arthur – though no tradition which would explain the association of his name with this spot survives. Llangollen is a natural point of entry from Cheshire into Wales, Arthur's country, and a slumber-legend is sometimes said to be attached to this landmark.

SJ 224470   OS 117
3 miles N of Llangollen, reached from an unclassified road turning NE off the A542

Pillar of Eliseg, Llangollen

In Valle Crucis ('Valley of the Cross'), which takes its name from a beautiful and now ruinous thirteenth-century Cistercian abbey, is an even more ancient religious memorial, the Pillar of Eliseg. It is the broken shaft of a cross erected to the memory of Eliseg king of Powys in the early ninth century. (Powys comprised north-east Wales, part of east–central Wales and the western part of Shropshire.) The cross bears a Latin genealogy of Eliseg which is now illegible but which was deciphered in the seventeenth century. Amongst Eliseg's ancestors is Vortigern, the British king who first invited the English Hengist and Horsa to help him fight the Picts, only to have Hengist and Horsa betray him. The story is told by the great Anglo-Saxon historian Bede, and much embroidered by Geoffrey of Monmouth, who creates the Arthurian association by causing Vortigern to discover Merlin.

SJ 202445 OS 117
2 miles N of Llangollen, just E of the A542

Dinas Bran, or Castell Dinas Bran, Llangollen

Dinas Bran is a fine Iron Age fortification with a medieval castle set within, on the bare hill-top. The mountain is called after Bran, a Celtic hero or god, who has an indirect association with Arthur – through his severed head. No house was large enough for Bran; he crossed the sea to Ireland by wading; he carried an army on his back across the Shannon; above all, he possessed a magic cauldron, which regenerated the cut-up bodies of men thrown into it. He was eventually killed by a poisoned spear lodged in his foot, and his severed head became a talisman for all satisfactions, like the Grail, of which the severed head may be in part a forerunner. The Welsh Triad of the 'Three Fortunate Concealments' refers to the burial of Bran's head in the White Hill in London (see THE WHITE TOWER).

Another influence on the Grail legend may come from Bran's horn. Just as when the Grail appeared all present were satisfied with food and drink, so Bran's horn was a horn of plenty. A Welsh list of the Thirteen Treasures of Britain, surviving in late medieval manuscripts, says of this horn that it provided all the food and drink one desired.

SJ 222431   OS 117
Reached by turning E off the A542 1 mile N of Llangollen

Castellmarch

A Welsh Triad of uncertain but early date tells a strange story of the Three Mighty Swineherds of Britain. One was Drystan, who guarded the swine of March (the Welsh form of the name Mark) while the real swineherd went off to ask Essyllt, who must be an early version of Iseult, to come to a meeting with Drystan. This is obviously an early primitive version of the story of Tristan's obsessive love for the wife of his uncle, King Mark of Cornwall. The story developed into one of the most famous love-stories of all time; Tristan himself came to be closely associated with Arthur's knights. Tristan's origin seems as Welsh as Arthur's, and Arthur himself is mentioned in the Triad as trying to steal one of the pigs, so the association between Arthur and Tristan is very early.

March is also the Welsh word for 'horse', and in Wales and Brittany a folktale circulated for several centuries about King March having horse's ears. He killed anyone who discovered his secret deformity, which led to a high death-rate among royal barbers, but in the end he gave up trying to conceal it because the very reeds which grew where the barbers were buried whispered the secret. The horse's ears –which relate to the classical story of King Midas, who had ass's ears –were soon dropped from the story as it moved into more courtly circles, but King Mark remained a rather ridiculous, as well as a dangerous and sinister, figure. Other variants of the horse's ears story, in association with persons whose name means 'horse', have been traced in Ireland, Wales and Brittany.

At some period a belief grew up that the site of Castellmarch, now occupied by the seventeenth-century private house of our picture, was where the original March lived. Maybe the name, 'horse castle', existed before the story, especially since March or Mark, and Tristan, are normally associated with Cornwall. The original story, however, seems very characteristic of Welsh folktale.

SH 314296   OS 123
Near the S coast of the Lleyn Peninsula, 1 mile N of Abersoch on the A499

River Nyfer

Rivers are boundaries, crossing-places and meeting-places, imaginatively significant spots for battles and confrontations. The River Nyfer appears in the Welsh story of 'Culhwch and Olwen' (*Introduction*, p. 8) on the route of Arthur's pursuit of the wild boar Twrch Trwyth, who landed at Port Cleis in Dyfed (Pembrokeshire) and ravaged the countryside. Arthur and his men chased him down both sides of the River Nyfer, until the boar stood at bay and killed many men before he was himself wounded and had to take to further flight.

SN 113373   OS 145
The river flows S of the A487 between Cardigan and Fishguard; an unclassified road from Croswell to Newport (Dyfed) runs beside the river

Arthur's Quoit, Pentre Ifan

Several Bronze Age (4000–2000 B.C.) burial-chambers, now denuded of the earth that once covered them, are called after Arthur. The one at Pentre Ifan in Dyfed is perhaps the best preserved and most dramatic. It is called Arthur's Quoit, though without any story known to attach to it, thus illustrating the dominance of the image of Arthur, vaguely conceived of as a folkloric giant hero. Such chambers create a real sense of the mysterious mighty past. (See also TRETHEVY QUOIT.)

SN 099370   OS 145
10 miles E of Fishguard, reached from an unclassified road turning S off the A487

Bosherston Fishponds

The long, winding lake south of Pembroke was once an arm of the sea, and perhaps the closeness of the coast of Dyfed led someone to claim this as the lake into which Sir Bedivere eventually, with such reluctance, threw Excalibur (see LOOE POOL).

SR 975946   OS 158
5 miles S of Pembroke, reached from the village of Bosherston on an unclassified road S of the B4319

St Govan's Chapel

St Govan's Chapel (illustrated opposite and overleaf) is one of those remarkable chapels that Celtic saints liked to build into the cliffs just above the sea. (There is another, similarly situated, on the Mull of Galloway.) The boundary of earth and sea and sky is a place for spiritual and, indeed, physical adventure, for access is difficult. Life must have been hard and uncomfortable, leading to, or deriving from, an intense spirituality.

The tiny chapel is by some claimed to be the hermitage of a sixth-century Irish monk, St Govan. When pursued by pirates he fled into a cleft in the rock, which closed, and thus concealed him from his enemies. When he emerged he established his chapel.

The Benedictine *Book of Saints* (1947) mentions only one St Govan, wife of King Tewdrig of Glamorgan. In any case, so little is known of Govan that he seems to have become confused with the Arthurian knight Gawain, and both saint and knight have been reputed to lie beneath the altar of the chapel. The twelfth-century historian William of Malmesbury may have been thus misled when he claimed that Gawain's tomb was in Pembrokeshire.

SR 967930   OS 158
On the coast 6 miles S of Pembroke, reached by an unclassified road from Bosherston

Roman Amphitheatre, Caerleon

Caerleon, on the River Usk near Newport, Gwent, was a fine Roman city, and we know from Giraldus (*Introduction*, p. 18) that in the twelfth century the ruins were remarkably extensive. They showed a degree of civilised luxury – for example, central heating and baths –quite untypical of contemporary medieval life. Geoffrey of Monmouth must have known these impressive ruins, since presumably (his name suggests) he grew up nearby. He describes how an early king, Belinus, founded the city called Kaerusc, and how it was renamed the City of the Legions. It is clear that Caerleon is meant. He goes on to tell how glorious this city became in Arthur's time – rich with buildings, full of ceremonies and festivities – in a way which foreshadows later writers' treatment of Camelot. (Geoffrey himself never uses the name Camelot for the seat of Arthur's court.) Guinevere fled here when Arthur returned to Britain to avenge her adultery with Mordred, and, according to Geoffrey, became a nun here in the church of Julius the Martyr. This all seems due to Geoffrey's richly inventive imagination playing over the splendid ruins. The amphitheatre became. at some time covered in earth and known as Arthur's Round Table (*Introduction*, p. 19), but it is now excavated.

Caerleon also has a slumber-legend, according to which a farmer, guided by a man in a three-cornered hat, came to a cave in which a thousand soldiers of Arthur were sleeping until Wales should need them. After leaving the cave, the farmer was sworn to secrecy for a year and a day, and he was subsequently unable to find the place again.

ST 339906   OS 171
2 miles NE of Newport (Gwent), on the B4236 beside the River Usk

Craig y Dinas

Above this enchanting spot of waterfalls and streams, the confluence of the Rivers Mellte and Sychryd, rises the splendid 'Rock of the Fortress', to which is attached one of the most elaborate of the Arthurian slumber-legends. A Welshman is led back to his native land from London by a stranger who promises to show him where treasure is hidden, and is introduced into the cave within the rock, where the king and his knights lie sleeping, with much gold. The Welshman is told that he can take as much gold as he likes but, if he should awaken the knights by ringing a bell which hangs in the cave, he must tell them to continue sleeping. Despite a warning to the contrary, the Welshman squanders the wealth which he thus successfully acquires, and later returns to the cave for more. Accidentally ringing the bell, he forgets what he is supposed to say to the awakened knights and is caught and beaten. He lives poor and crippled, and is never able to find the entrance again.

SN 915080   OS 160
18 miles NE of Swansea, reached from the B4242

The Brecon Beacons

Giraldus Cambrensis (*Introduction*, p. 18), in the late twelfth century, describes Arthur's Chair as formed by two peaks of the Brecon Beacons and the dip between them; and the Welsh scholar John David Rhys, writing in 1592, also refers to 'Arthur's Hill-Top'. Here folklore, as so often (for example with Arthur's numerous quoits), playfully imagines Arthur as a giant, associating outstanding features in a familiar, humanising and unserious way with a great name.

SO 012216   OS 160
5 miles S of Brecon and E of the A470

Arthur's Stone, Hereford

This is one of a number of ancient burial-chambers, up to five thousand years old, made of great slabs of rock from which the earth has long since been washed away, to which Arthur's name, and sometimes a legend, has been attached. Such ancient monuments, in appearance neither completely man-made nor completely natural, often remote, and having an intrinsic air of mystery and the sacredness of death about them, stimulate the imagination. In this case the huge capstone with its indentations has attracted some common motifs. It was thought to mark Arthur's fight with a giant, whose elbows made indentations as he lay dying against the stone. Alternatively, they were made by Arthur's knees as he prayed, or by his fingers as he played at quoits. Other stories see the stones as marking the grave of some great person.

The very early reference in Nennius to Arthur killing his own son (*Introduction*, p. 11) is also associated with Hereford.

SO 318431   OS 161
15 miles E of Hereford, reached from an unclassified road turning NE off the B4348

The North of England and Scotland

For all the powerful effect of Welsh imagination on the story of Arthur, there are numerous associations (*Introduction*, p. 22) with the north of England and with Scotland. There is a group of references in the western Lowlands, which together with Cumbria once formed the Celtic kingdom of Strathclyde: for example, DUMBARTON ROCK is near the town of Dumbarton, which in a record of 1367 was called *castrum Arthuri* ('the fortification of Arthur').

There is another group of associations in the eastern Lowlands, which in ancient times were not divided from the north of England. This region made up Geoffrey of Monmouth's kingdom of Lothian, whose King Loth in his account was Mordred's father. Edinburgh has its ARTHUR'S SEAT, and it was from the region of Edinburgh that the Gododdin set out on their fatal raid into Northumberland commemorated in the poem now called *The Gododdin*, which gives us one of our earliest references to Arthur (*Introduction*, p. 10).

In Northumberland, on Hadrian's Wall, SEWINGSHIELDS CRAGS has a slumber-legend and an Arthur's Chair, from which, one story has it, Arthur threw a boulder at Guinevere on Queen's Crags nearby. Here is a touch of the primitive Celtic Arthur. At Cummings Cross Arthur's sons were said to attack guests returning from Arthur's palace and rob them of the gifts Arthur had given them.

Over on the east coast of Northumberland the magnificent castles of BAMBURGH and ALNWICK were associated with Lancelot's castle, Joyous Gard, Malory remarking that 'Some men say it was Alnwick and some men say it was Bamburgh.' RICHMOND CASTLE had acquired its slumber-legend by the nineteenth century.

In the north two places are named Arthur's Round Table. One is at MAYBURGH, on ancient circular mounds of Bronze or Iron Age origin; another is by Stirling Castle, and is more usually called 'the King's Knot'. The latter is a pleasant invention of fifteenth- and sixteenth-century writers and courtiers, during a creative period for Arthurian legend. For the most part, however, late medieval Scottish writers took a poor view of Arthur and were inclined to side with Mordred (*Introduction*, p. 21).

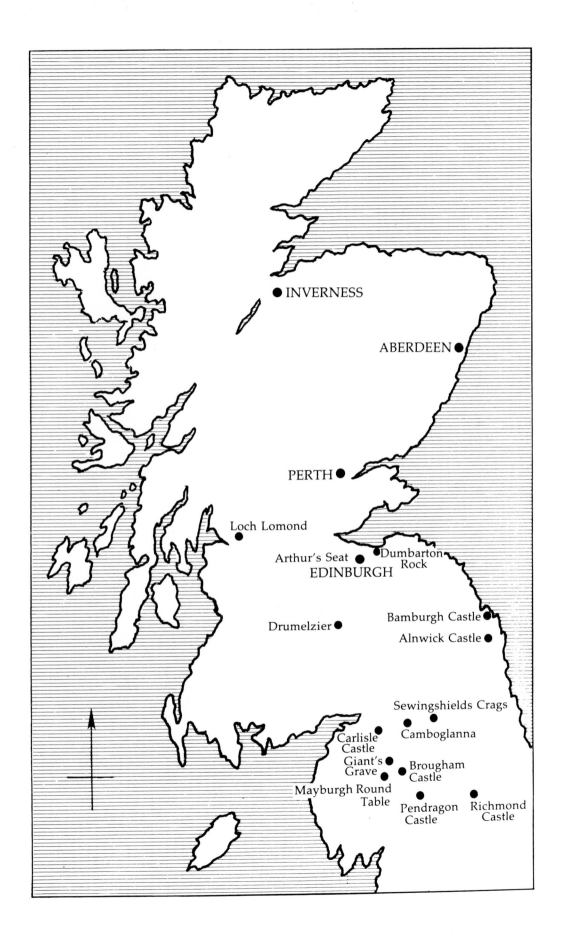

INVERNESS

ABERDEEN

PERTH

Loch Lomond

Arthur's Seat
EDINBURGH

Dumbarton
Rock

Drumelzier

Bamburgh Castle

Alnwick Castle

Sewingshields Crags

Camboglanna

Carlisle
Castle
Giant's
Grave

Brougham
Castle

Mayburgh Round
Table

Pendragon
Castle

Richmond
Castle

Richmond Castle

Founded in 1071, the Norman castle of Richmond towers over the River Swale in a beautiful valley. It is one of the earliest stone-built castles in England, and many parts of its structure, including the walls, still date from Norman times. A footpath, the Castle Walk, runs round the castle; the cliffs below it form a magnificent natural fortress, and there are glorious views over the Swale valley (see overleaf).

The site has a slumber-legend, of which the unadmirable hero, this time, is one Potter Thompson. He found a tunnel running into the hillside (perhaps from the Castle Walk), and discovered Arthur and his knights asleep round a table on which lay a sword and a horn. He fled as the sleepers began to stir, and a voice called:

> Potter Thompson, Potter Thompson
> If thou hadst either drawn
> The sword or blown the horn
> Thou'dst been the luckiest man
> That ever yet was born.

NZ 172006   OS 92
12 miles SW of Darlington, on the A6108

Pendragon Castle

Amongst hills, between the fine River Eden and the road, lie the ruins of Pendragon Castle, built, according to tradition, by Utherpendragon, father of Arthur. In fact, the small castle dates from the twelfth century and was built by Hugh de Morville, one of the murderers of Archbishop Thomas à Beckett. Hugh had strong Arthurian interests; we are told by Ulrich von Zatzikhoven, the Swiss author of the earliest romance on Sir Lancelot, that Hugh de Morville gave him a book in a foreign language (presumably French) which he translated into German. Hugh was at that time (the 1190s) a hostage for Richard the Lionhearted on the Continent, but, though of Norman origin, was a native English speaker. His life was almost as full of dramatic event as an Arthurian tale: besides his involvement in the murder of the archbishop, his wife fell in love with a young man who resisted her and whom she then tried to get killed by her husband. It was presumably Hugh's choice to call his castle by a romantic Arthurian name; perhaps he thought of himself as a kind of Uther. Malory refers to a Castle of Pendragon owned by Sir Bryan de Les Illes, who kept many prisoners in it. Sir Lancelot deprived Sir Bryan of possession and gave it to the brave young knight nicknamed La Cote Male Tayle.

A legend tells that Utherpendragon wished to divert the nearby River Eden in order to make a moat round his new castle of Pendragon. He failed, of course; hence the derisive rhyme, asserting the power of nature,

> Let Utherpendragon do what he can
> Eden will run where Eden ran.

Here the river is viewed from the castle ruins.

NY 782026   OS 91
The castle lies 4 miles S of Kirkby Stephen, between the B6259 and the River Eden

Brougham Castle

Brougham Castle occupies an ancient site and is close to what was once a large Roman fort, but itself dates from the twelfth century. This romantic spot has attracted a legend, unrecorded elsewhere, that a giant lived in a cave in the grounds and was killed by Sir Lancelot. It is very rare for Lancelot to get into folk-legend, and this suggests a late date for the origin of the story. Even Malory, the most ardent literary admirer of Lancelot, knows nothing of Brougham Castle or of Lancelot as a giant-killer, though Arthur himself and other heroes achieved such adventures.

NY 537290   OS 90
1 mile E of Penrith, on an unclassified road turning S off the A66 to Appleby

Mayburgh Round Table

Like several other 'Round Tables', the one at Mayburgh is an ancient earthwork, in this case probably Bronze Age (about 4000 B.C.). It illustrates the way outstanding features attract interesting names, and the power of the idea of the Round Table. Forming a piquant contrast with the unassuming village nearby, it recalls the long turbulent history of the land so vividly evoked by Arthurian story itself.

NY 523284   OS 90
1 mile S of Penrith, SW of the junction of the A6 and B5320

The Giant's Grave, Penrith

The picturesque Giant's Grave in the churchyard of St Andrew's is composed of several tenth-century monuments, which may have been rearranged as late as the rebuilding of the church in 1772. However, there is a local legend of indeterminate date that the stones mark the grave of one huge man, the sixth-century Celtic King Owein, who is mentioned in early Welsh poetry and transformed in later French romance into Ywain, who became one of Arthur's knights. As such he is called 'Ewan Caesarius', and described as a great boar-hunter.

The proximity of other Arthurian sites (see BROUGHAM CASTLE and MAYBURGH ROUND TABLE) may have suggested the Arthurian associations here.

NY 516302   OS 90
St Andrew's Church is near the junction of Devonshire St and the Market Square in the centre of Penrith

Carlisle Castle

There seems to be no folk-legend of Arthur at Carlisle, and Geoffrey of Monmouth only briefly mentions the town as founded by an early king, Leil – contemporary, he says, with Solomon. Carlisle creeps into the French romances, however, and Malory, either following them or independently, introduces Carlisle as one of Arthur's castles and places of residence. It is here that he places Lancelot's return of Guinevere to Arthur after her rescue from the stake and her subseqent sojourn with him at Joyous Gard.

The town, just to the south of the western end of Hadrian's Wall, was a Roman settlement, and became an important border fortress in medieval times. The castle was founded in 1092 and has an impressive Norman keep. Being well known in such fighting times, it figures in a number of ballads; and in the fifteenth and sixteenth centuries it developed other Arthurian associations in the popular mind, with Sir Gawain as hero. A late ballad called 'The Marriage of Sir Gawaine' begins:

> King Arthur lives in merry Carlisle
> And seemly is to see
> And there with him Queen Guenevere
> That bride so bright of blee.

Another poem, 'The Carl of Carlisle', tells of a giant whom Gawain releases from a spell. There was clearly a northern tradition of Gawain as a hero, the greatest example being one of the best poems written in English, the fourteenth-century *Sir Gawain and the Green Knight*, though the setting of that is probably Derbyshire.

NY 398562   OS 85
Just N of the centre of Carlisle

Camboglanna Roman Fort, Birdoswald

On the magnificent Roman defence system of Hadrian's Wall, high up over the River Irthing, stand the ruins of a substantial fort known to the Welsh as Camlann and to the Scots as Camboglanna. If Arthur was originally a king of Dalriada, as is not impossible (*Introduction*, p. 22), then this could well be the historical site of the battle between Arthur and Medrawd (Mordred). The wall, which had been built a century or two before the battle (but which is scarcely mentioned in Arthurian legends), remains to remind us of the warring kingdoms that once rent this land.

NY 615663   OS 86
16 miles NE of Carlisle, reached by an unclassified road turning S off the B6318 1 mile W of Gilsland

Sewingshields Crags
(overleaf)

Hadrian's Wall surmounts the hills dividing the kingdom of Lothian. The greatest Roman settlement is what is now called Housesteads Fort, from which the wall can be seen crawling up to Sewingshields Crags, a beautiful cliff-like formation, near which Sewingshields Castle once stood. A slumber-legend of the usual kind was attached to the castle. A local farmer came by chance upon the entrance to a cave beneath the castle, and within found not only Arthur and his knights, but a sword, a garter and a horn. He cut the garter with the sword, whereupon Arthur woke and said:

> O woe betide the evil day
> On which this witless wight was born
> Who drew the sword, the garter cut,
> But never blew the bugle-horn.

He then fell asleep once more, the farmer retreated, and the cave-entrance was never found again.

Nearby are limestone outcrops called King's Crags and Queen's Crags, and on King's Crags is another Arthur's Chair. The story goes that Arthur and Guinevere sat on their crags and quarrelled, and Arthur threw a boulder at Guinevere; it bounced off her comb and now lies between them, still visibly bearing the marks of the comb.

NY 799700   OS 87
12 miles NW of Hexham, reached by turning N off the B6318

Alnwick Castle

Alnwick Castle is mentioned by Malory, with Bamburgh Castle, as the possible Joyous Gard of Sir Lancelot. Malory is the only writer to associate these two castles with Lancelot, perhaps because he knew them both from his own experience. (For details, see BAMBURGH CASTLE.)

Alnwick Castle remains inhabited and must always have been a most imposing place. The outer walls date from the twelfth century, and the impressive gatehouse, built about 1440, could have been known to Malory. The beautiful grounds were designed in the eighteenth century, and the castle itself was substantially restored in 1854, but it retains its medieval style and splendour.

NU 187136   OS 81
Midway between Newcastle and Berwick, just off the A1

Bamburgh Castle
(overleaf)

On a romantic site on a low hill by the seaside stands the splendid castle of Bamburgh, one of Malory's two possible sites for Lancelot's Joyous Gard. Lancelot offered it as a haven to Tristan and Iseult when they fled together from King Mark; and when he himself had rescued Guinevere from the stake at which she was condemned to be burned for her adultery with him, they stayed together at Joyous Gard. Eventually, when Lancelot had to deliver up the queen to Arthur again, he renamed his castle Dolorous Gard.

An English king had set up a wooden fortress on the site of Bamburgh Castle in 547, and there are historical and folkloric associations with early English Christianity in the person of St Aidan. The imposing red sandstone keep was built about 1164, but the rest of the castle has been heavily restored, especially in the late nineteenth century. Malory himself may have served at the sieges of Bamburgh and ALNWICK in the Wars of the Roses during Christmas and New Year 1462–3, and thus have come to know these mighty strongholds.

NU 183350   OS 75
5 miles SE of Holy Island, on the Northumbrian coast, reached by turning E off the A1 onto the B1342 or B1341

Drumelzier Church

Merlin is the type of the old wise man, magician, prophet, shape-changer, who yet falls into madness, because of grief for his friends and king killed in battle, or through becoming infatuated with a girl. He seems to have been invented by Geoffrey of Monmouth, but the creation soon flowered in other minds and became a more general possession, descending eventually to folktales centring on Drumelzier (pronounced Drumelyay) on the Scottish border by the River Tweed. Geoffrey wrote a *Life of Merlin,* drawing on Celtic tales – perhaps to give force, by inventing a suitable character as speaker, to some obscure anonymous prophecies, already in circulation, of supposedly forthcoming political events. References in Welsh poems to a Welsh bard Myrddin probably all arise from Geoffrey's account.

Legend has it that, after the death of Arthur, Merlin stirred up conflict between Celts and Britons. The side he supported suffered severe losses, and, crazed with grief and guilt, he ran wild in 'the Caledonian Forest' (now bare hills) and was stoned to death by shepherds as a pagan, though he had recently been baptised on the 'altarstone' now preserved at Drumelzier Church. According to another version, he was chased by the shepherds, jumped off a cliff above the Tweed, caught his feet in salmon-stakes, hung head-downward in the river, and so was drowned, being buried in Drumelzier Church. Later romances had him shut up in a cave somewhere by the maiden Nimue, with whom he was madly in love, after she had tricked him into telling her the secret of his powers of enchantment. The actual stories are probably based on those about a now forgotten Lailocen, a madman who appears in various lives of the Scottish St Kentigern. Nowadays Merlin attracts more literary attention than ever, but folk-legends are scanty; why they should have become attached to Drumelzier is not clear.

NT 135343   OS 72
28 miles S of Edinburgh on the B712, 1½ miles E of its junction with the A701

Dumbarton Rock

Dumbarton is associated with Arthur as *castrum Arthuri* ('the fort of Arthur') in a parliamentary record of King David II of Scotland in 1367. Highland folktales also make this the birthplace of Mordred, whom later Scottish tradition favoured against the English tyrant Arthur (*Introduction*, p. 21). Dumbarton's ancient name was Alclud (or Alclyde), and as such it appears in Celtic sources and in Geoffrey of Monmouth's *History*. Several unconvincing attempts have been made to locate here various of the battles mentioned by Nennius in the ninth century.

The rock, strikingly situated on the River Clyde, is of volcanic basalt. Its dramatic shape, and its boundary position between land and sea, are calculated to attract folktale, such as that which recounts how the Devil, wishing to expel St Patrick from Scotland, had him chased by witches. The saint escaped by boat, whereupon the angry witches tore up part of a hill, and threw it at him. It fell short and remains as Dumbarton Rock.

NS 400745   OS 64
15 miles NW of Glasgow on a rocky headland jutting into the Clyde from Dumbarton

Arthur's Seat, Edinburgh

In the Black Book of Carmarthen, poem xxxi (composed in Welsh, probably before the eleventh century) has a dialogue between Arthur and his gatekeeper. Arthur approaches the gate, and the gatekeeper asks, 'Who is there?' Arthur replies, 'Arthur and Cai the Fair.' 'Who travels with you?' The answer is an extraordinary assortment of warriors – among them two who 'were helping at the Eidyn [i.e. Edinburgh] on the borders'. The 'mountain of Eidyn' is also mentioned as a place where Arthur 'fought with Dogheads', though who these were is unknown.

Edinburgh, in the kingdom of Lothian, was, as we have seen (*Introduction, p. 00*), in the region whence came the Gododdin (the Celts whose raid down to Catterick was celebrated in the poem which gives us one of our earliest references to Arthur), and it became one of the earliest centres of Arthurian legend. Geoffrey of Monmouth refers to the founding of Edinburgh at the same time as Alclud (Dumbarton) and makes it contemporary with the reign of the biblical King David. He calls Edinburgh the castle of Mount Agned, 'which is now called the Maiden's Castle and the Dolorous Mountain', without giving reasons for these names. Agned, however, is the name of the mountain given as the site of Arthur's eleventh battle by Nennius. Later French romances occasionally refer to Edinburgh and the Castle of Maidens, but clearly with no direct knowledge.

The ancient knowledge of Arthur seems to have moved with the Celts to Wales, and the magnificent steep hill – the cone of an extinct volcano – called Arthur's Seat probably owes less to ancient Celtic legend and medieval literary references than to the general penchant for naming outstanding natural features, especially hills with a saddleback effect, somebody's 'Seat'. The name 'Arthur's Seat' is recorded for this rock from the fifteenth century.

NT 275729   OS 66
Best approached from Holyrood Palace, 1 mile E of Edinburgh Castle

Loch Lomond
(*overleaf*)

Loch Lomond, the largest lake in Britain, lies north of Dumbarton, and is vividly if inaccurately described by Geoffrey of Monmouth. In his *History* Geoffrey represents Arthur victoriously pursuing the Scots and Picts on to the islands of Loch Lomond. Of these, he says, there are sixty, providing sixty crags and sixty eagles' nests. The eagles flock together once a year and foretell any prodigious event to come by emitting a scream in unison. Arthur collected a fleet and starved the fugitive Scots and Picts to death in their thousands.

Under this account lies the primitive sense of the mysterious symbolism of pools and lakes, seen in the eighth-century English poem *Beowulf,* and elaborated by the English poet Layamon when he wrote his poem *The Brut,* which derives from Geoffrey's *History.*

NS 380900   OS 56
About 15 miles NW of Glasgow, parallel with the A82

Bibliography

The huge number of works on Arthurian legend is noted for scholars by C. E. Pickford and Rex Last, *The Arthurian Bibliography* (Cambridge: D. S. Brewer, 1981, with supplements). In writing the present book I have relied chiefly on the following:

Arthurian Literature in the Middle Ages, edited by R. S. Loomis (Oxford: Clarendon Press, 1959).

Ashe, Geoffrey, *A Guidebook to Arthurian Britain* (London: Longman, 1980; paperback, Wellingborough: The Aquarian Press, 1983).

Barber, Richard, *The Figure of Arthur* (London: Longman, 1972).

Chambers, E. K., *Arthur of Britain* (London: Sidgwick and Jackson, 1972).

Fairbairn, N. and M. Cyprien, *A Traveller's Guide to the Kingdoms of Arthur* (London: Evans Brothers Ltd, 1983).

Rhys, J., *The Arthurian Legend* (Oxford: Clarendon Press, 1891).

Texts (apart from those quoted in Chambers, etc., above):

Geoffrey of Monmouth, *The History of the Kings of Britain,* translated with an introduction by Lewis Thorpe (Harmondsworth: Penguin Books, 1966).

The Mabinogion, translated by Gwyn Jones and Thomas Jones, Everyman's Library (London: J. M. Dent, 1949).

Sir Thomas Malory, *The Works,* edited by E. Vinaver (Oxford: Clarendon Press, 1947; second edition 1967, reprinted with corrections 1973).

Index of names